❋ NEWFANGLED ❋
PIECING
Faster & Easier

Cathy BUSCH

American Quilter's Society

PO Box 3290 • Paducah, KY 42002-3290
Fax 270-898-1173 • email: orders@AQSquilt.com

Located in Paducah, Kentucky, the American Quilter's Society (AQS) is dedicated to promoting the accomplishments of today's quilters. Through its publications and events, AQS strives to honor today's quiltmakers and their work and to inspire future creativity and innovation in quiltmaking.

EXECUTIVE BOOK EDITOR: ELAINE H. BRELSFORD
BOOK EDITOR: LINDA BAXTER LASCO
COPY EDITOR: CHRYSTAL ABHALTER
ILLUSTRATIONS: CATHY BUSCH
GRAPHIC DESIGN: SARAH BOZONE
COVER DESIGN: MICHAEL BUCKINGHAM
QUILT PHOTOGRAPHY: CHARLES R. LYNCH

Additional copies of this book may be ordered from the American Quilter's Society, PO Box 3290, Paducah, KY 42002-3290, or online at www.AmericanQuilter.com.

Text and illustrations © 2014, Author, Cathy Busch
Artwork © 2014, American Quilter's Society

American Quilter's Society
PO Box 3290 • Paducah, KY 42002-3290
Fax 270-898-1173 • email: orders@AQSquilt.com

Library of Congress Cataloging-in-Publication Data

Busch, Cathy.
  Newfangled piecing / by Cathy Busch.
    pages cm
  Includes bibliographical references and index.
  ISBN 978-1-60460-108-4 (alkaline paper)
  1. Quilting--Patterns. 2. Patchwork--Patterns. I. American Quilter's Society. II. Title.
  TT835.B885 2014
  746.46'041--dc23

                              2014002715

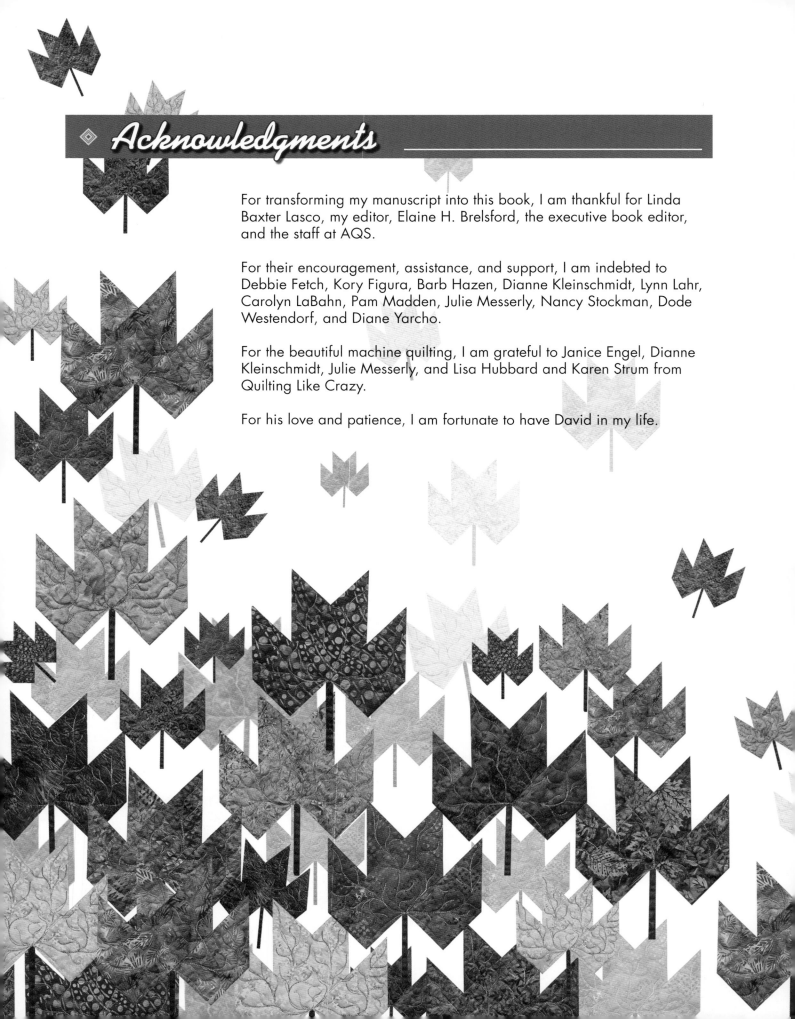

Acknowledgments

For transforming my manuscript into this book, I am thankful for Linda Baxter Lasco, my editor, Elaine H. Brelsford, the executive book editor, and the staff at AQS.

For their encouragement, assistance, and support, I am indebted to Debbie Fetch, Kory Figura, Barb Hazen, Dianne Kleinschmidt, Lynn Lahr, Carolyn LaBahn, Pam Madden, Julie Messerly, Nancy Stockman, Dode Westendorf, and Diane Yarcho.

For the beautiful machine quilting, I am grateful to Janice Engel, Dianne Kleinschmidt, Julie Messerly, and Lisa Hubbard and Karen Strum from Quilting Like Crazy.

For his love and patience, I am fortunate to have David in my life.

◆ Contents

◈ *Introduction*

For hundreds of years, quilters pieced their blocks by tracing templates onto fabric, cutting the pieces with scissors, and sewing the pieces together. Advances in tools changed this laborious process. With the use of rotary cutters and acrylic rulers, quilters could cut strips, sew them together, cut the resulting strip-sets, and then construct their blocks. The era of strip piecing had begun. *Newfangled Piecing: Faster & Easier* is my approach to further speed up the process of quiltmaking.

My inspiration came from a workshop and two non-quilters.

I took a workshop for a Christmas quilt. The quilt was made of alternating Star and pieced Tree blocks. The Star was made from 12 half-square triangles. What I saw was a Variable Star block. That's when I realized life's too short to make that many half-square triangles for a Christmas quilt. I could use an alternative and faster technique instead (a square in-a-square center surrounded by flying geese). The experience taught me to look more critically at blocks with an eye toward simpler and easier construction.

Yogi Berra is my first non-quilter inspiration. Besides baseball, Yogi is well known for his somewhat puzzling statements. These include, "It ain't over till it's over and "Baseball is ninety percent mental. The other half is physical." Giving directions to his home, he would say, "When you come to a fork in the road, take it." Yogi lived on a circular drive. Taking either road would get you to his house. I realized this quote also applies to quilting. There are many forks in the road (techniques) that will get you home (to the block or unit you desire).

Construction of half-square triangles illustrates such a fork in the road. Quilters can assemble this unit composed of two right triangles with specialty rulers, using two squares of fabric, drawing grids on fabric, using papers with drawn sewing and cutting lines, or with fusible web printed with sewing and cutting lines. All these methods, and probably more, are designed to make a half-square triangle. Selecting the most efficient method for a given project is a valuable skill and one I hope you will learn from this book.

The second inspiration is celebrity chef Jamie Oliver. His philosophy is to reduce cooking to its bare essentials by using simple ingredients and techniques. In quilting, I've discovered that many traditional pieced blocks can also be reduced to their barest elements.

When these ideas came together—using the most efficient construction methods and selecting the simplest units—I found I was using my time and materials more effectively. I've developed four strategies to help me when I'm reading a pattern. I look for ways to:
1. Eliminate seams
2. Substitute units
3. Identify alternate methods of block construction
4. See the big picture.

Once you adopt these strategies and use them alone or in combination, your piecework will be quicker, easier, and more accurate.

◈ Strategies

An important first step in quiltmaking is reading the pattern directions. You need to understand what is required and how to achieve the desired result. Reading the pattern also provides the opportunity to decide if there are ways to simplify the process.

I learned the lesson the hard way. I was making a quilt designed to use 5" charm squares. Not having a ready stash of 5" squares, I decided to use fat quarters. Rather than read the directions, I cut 15 fat quarters into 240 charm squares. THEN I read the directions, which said to cut 80 charm squares into 4½" x 4½" squares, 80 charm squares into 4½" x 2½" rectangles, and the remaining charm squares into 2½" x 2½" squares. I was not a happy recutter. Two minutes of reading the directions would have saved me time as well as wear and tear on both my rotary cutter, shoulder, and ego.

Strategy 1: Eliminate Seams

Most patchwork blocks are classified by the number of units in the block. A Four-Patch block is made of four units set in two rows of two units each. A Nine-Patch block consists of nine units set in three rows of three units each. A Sixteen-Patch block has four rows of four units each. A Twenty-Five-Patch block has five rows of five units each.

The first thing to do when you look at a block is to identify any seams that can be eliminated. Why sew two identical squares together when you can use a rectangle? Why sew four small squares when you can use a larger square? The time and fabric saved by eliminating a seam in one block is saved again on each block in the quilt.

One of the first blocks I ever made was the Spool block.

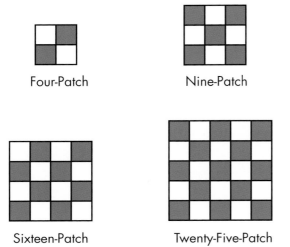

Four-Patch

Nine-Patch

Sixteen-Patch

Twenty-Five-Patch

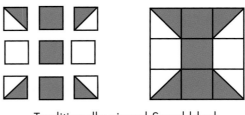

Traditionally pieced Spool block

It is a Nine-Patch block. The top and bottom rows are made from half-square triangles and a square. The middle row is made from three squares. To simplify the block, eliminate seams in the top and bottom rows by making a unit I call a flip-corner rectangle. The middle row can be made by cutting a pieced rectangle from a strip-set.

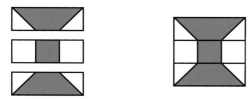

Newfangled Spool block

The number of seams is reduced from twelve to eight. Strip-piecing the center row eliminates two more seams from subsequent blocks.

Flip corners are made by positioning two fabrics right sides together, sewing a diagonal seam, and pressing the flip fabric toward the corner. There are two different methods for making flip corners—one with squares and one with triangles. See pages 21–23 for detailed instructions for both methods.

I refer to either right- or left-flip corners. When making flip corners it is important to pay attention to the direction of the flip. The right-flip corner flips toward the upper right corner of the base shape (either a square or rectangle) while a left-flip corner flips toward the upper left corner of the base shape.

Right Flip   Left Flip

In many traditional Nine-Patch blocks you can eliminate seams by using flip-corner rectangles as shown in the following before and after diagrams.

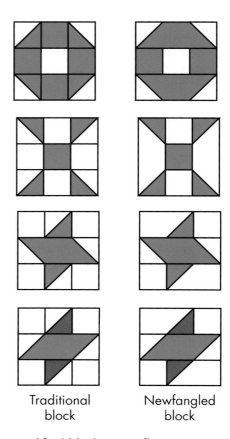

Traditional   Newfangled
block   block

Four simplified blocks using flip-corner rectangles

The Maple Leaf block is another example of eliminating half-square triangles (in the second and third rows) by making flip-corner rectangles.

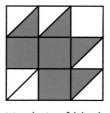
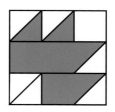

Maple Leaf block   Newfangled Maple
                       Leaf block

Traditionally, the Stretch Star is made from squares and half-square triangles. Eliminating seams reduces this block to four flip-corner rectangles, one double flip-corner square, and two corner squares.

Eliminating seams requires calculating the cut size of the replacement units. I realize that for many quilters "math" is a four-letter word. (Actually, it is a four-letter word for all quilters.) See page 94 for all the math you need, already calculated for you.

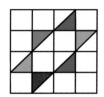
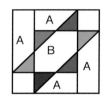

Stretch Star block   Newfangled Stretch
                          Star block

Strategy 2: Substitute Units

Once you've mastered eliminating seams, the next step is to look for ways to substitute units.

The block below is a Star block from that Christmas quilt workshop I took. The two-fabric block was made from twelve half-square triangles and four corner squares.

In another substitution example, use a square-in-a-square unit in the center of the Susannah block to replace four half-square triangles. To further ease construction, substitute rectangles from a two-fabric strip-set and a four-fabric strip-set for the sides and the top and bottom rows of the block, respectively.

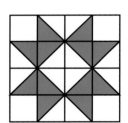

Traditionally pieced Star block

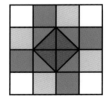

Traditionally pieced
Susannah block

I made one block and realized I could substitute a square-in-a-square for the block center. I could surround the center with four flying geese units and add four corner squares. By substituting units, the construction was quicker and easier.

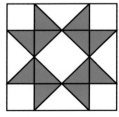

Newfangled
Star block

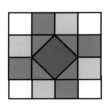

Newfangled
Susannah block

The square-in-a-square is common in many pieced blocks. Traditionally, four triangles are sewn around a center square. The calculations to determine the cut size of the center square and side triangles can be a bit tricky and seldom results "nice" numbers. Once the pieces are cut, sewn, and pressed, you cross your fingers and hope that the unit is square.

Traditionally pieced
square-in-a-square

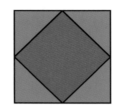
Newfangled
square-in-a-square

An easier way to accomplish the goal is to cut a square and add four flip corners. See page 27 for detailed cutting and sewing directions for flip-corner square in-a-square units.

Eliminating seams and substituting units often go hand-in-hand. Substituting flying geese for half-square triangles is another example. Whenever two half-square triangles are joined together with the same fabric forming a "goose body" triangle, I substitute a flying geese unit. The side triangle "wings" can be either the same or different fabrics.

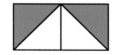
Two half-square triangles

Flying geese with same
color corners

Flying geese with
different color corners

In many scrap quilt patterns, two half-square triangles with different "goose body" fabrics are joined to make flying geese. I refer to them as flip-corner split rectangles. Make a strip-set from the two body fabrics, cut rectangle units from the strip-set, and add flip corners to the rectangles and geese fly off your sewing machine. See pages 24–26 for detailed cutting and sewing directions for flying geese units.

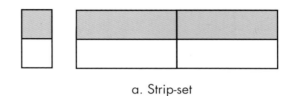
a. Strip-set

b. First corner flip

c. Finished unit

Flying geese from two-fabric strip-set
rectangles with two flip corners

Another of my favorite substitutions is the parallelogram. Think of this unit as a flying goose with a broken wing. In flying geese, the corners on the same long side of the base rectangle are flipped. In a parallelogram, two opposite corners of the base rectangle are flipped.

Replacing two half-square
triangles with a parallelogram

When making parallelograms, you need to pay close attention to the slant of the seams.

- In a right-flip parallelogram, the flips are toward the upper right and lower left corners.
- In a left-flip parallelogram, the flips are toward the upper left and lower right corners.

Right-flip parallelogram   Left-flip parallelogram

The fabric used for the flip corners in a parallelogram can be the same or different. The center can also be made from two different fabrics (split parallelograms). You will quickly begin to recognize parallelograms in pieced blocks.

Parallelogram variations

Study the before and after diagrams to see how substituting parallelograms simplifies the blocks. See pages 26–27 for detailed instructions for cutting and sewing parallelograms.

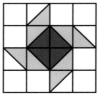

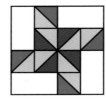 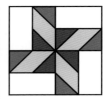

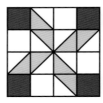 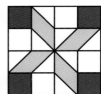

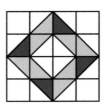 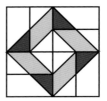

Traditional block   Newfangled block

Half-square triangles replaced with parallelograms

Strategy 3: Alternate Methods of Block Construction

As piecers, we tend to look at blocks as rows and columns. Traditionally, block construction consists of sewing units together to make rows, then joining the rows to make a block. Strategy Three has you looking for alternative ways to construct the block.

In a simple Pinwheel block, flip-corner rectangles replace half-square triangles. The flip-corner rectangle is joined to a background rectangle to make a quadrant. Four quadrants are then joined to make the block.

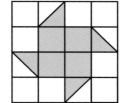

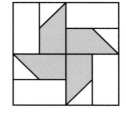

Construction by quadrants

These Sixteen-Patch blocks are symmetrical. Speed up your piecing by using quadrant construction.

Traditional block   Newfangled block

a. Join flying geese and strip-set rectangles to make quadrants.

b. Join flying geese and left-flip corner rectangles to make quadrants.

c. Join flying geese and parallelograms to make quadrants.

d. Join parallelograms and left-flip corner rectangles to make quadrants.

Another tool every quilter needs to know is partial seam construction. In this technique, only part of a seam is sewn to join the center unit of a block to one of the side units. The remaining side units are then added in a clockwise (or counterclockwise) fashion. After the last side unit is added, the initial seam is completed.

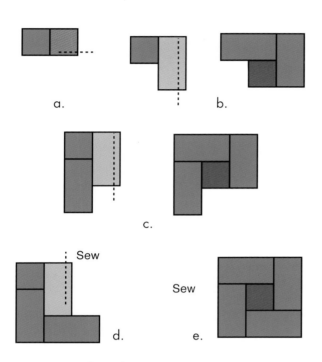

a.

b.

c.

Sew

d.

Sew

e.

Partial seam construction

a. Sew from the edge of the center of the square.
b. Sew the full seam of the next piece. Press away from the center square.
c. Turn the unit, add the next piece, and press.
d. Turn the unit, add the last piece, and press.
e. Complete the first seam.

There are two keys to successful partial seam construction. First, always press the seams away from the center square. This will make closing the final seam easier. The second is to pin not only on the seam edge but also on the adjacent edge. This helps keep the unit square.

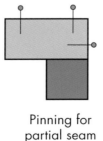

Pinning for partial seam success

The Ribbon Star block is a Nine-Patch block traditionally made from eight half-square triangles and a center square. To simplify the block, sew four flying geese OR four parallelograms counterclockwise around the center square using partial seam construction.

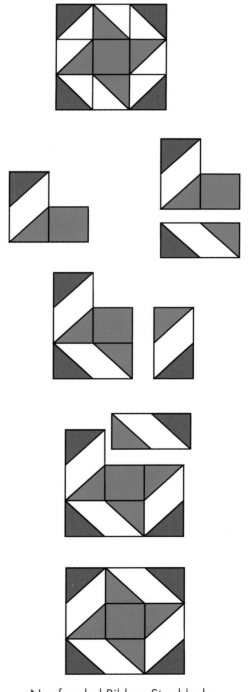

Newfangled Ribbon Star blocks

The Eccentric Star is another candidate for partial seam construction. You can replace the half-square triangles with either flying geese or parallelograms.

Using flying geese

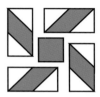

Using parallelograms

Two options for a newfangled Eccentric Star block

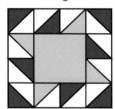

Traditional block

1. 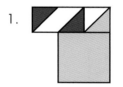 2.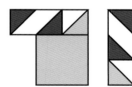

3.  4.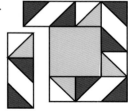

5.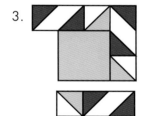

Combining substitution strategies and partial seam construction simplifies this block.

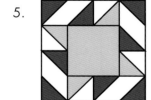

Newfangled block

Using block simplification strategies, you will see that there are often several ways to make the same block. See how quadrant or partial seam construction can be used in this block.

Traditional block

 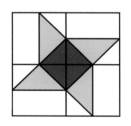

Newfangled block using flying geese and rectangles.

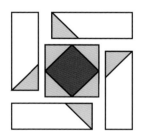 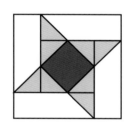

Newfangled block using square-in-a-square and left flip rectangles.

There can be more than one way to simplify a block.

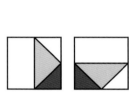
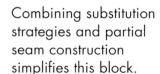

Strategy 4: See the Big Picture

Finally, look at the big picture and study the quilt as a whole. Many quilts are made without sashing. In an unsashed quilt, the blocks are set next to each other. This arrangement is common in both one-block and two-block quilts. In the following quilt, Sawtooth Star blocks with the same background fabric are joined in rows. The rows are then joined to make the quilt center.

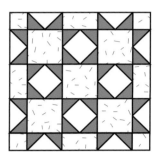

Same look, simplified construction

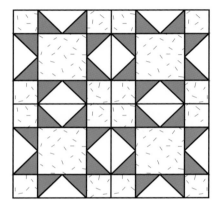

Traditional quilt construction with four Star blocks

When the background fabric is the same, rows of squares, rectangles, flying geese, and square-in-a-square units simplify the construction. The square-in-a-square units made the star points match perfectly.

Simplify the block, simplify the quilt. In this Stacked Star quilt, I could have just eliminated seams in the block and sewn the blocks together. Seeing the big picture, I made the quilt in columns of stars rather than rows of blocks.

Traditional
block

Newfangled
block

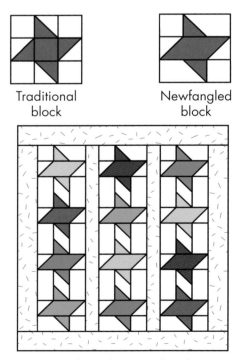

Construction by columns rather than rows

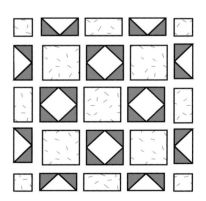

Simplify the Cypress block by replacing half-square triangles with square-in-a-square units and flying geese.

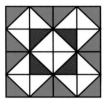

Traditional
Cypress block

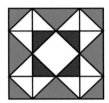

Newfangled
Cypress block

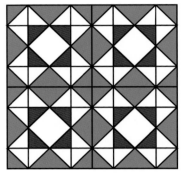

Traditional quilt construction

To simplify a quilt made from Cypress blocks, I made columns of alternating square-in-a-square units and hourglass units. Flying geese were used around the outside to complete the quilt.

Newfangled arrangement

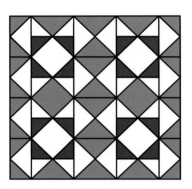

Newfangled simplified quilt construction

These four strategies, used alone or in combination, provide opportunities to simplify your quilting. Time spent considering these strategies will be rewarded with time saved in fabric cutting and quilt construction.

◆ Basic Techniques

When you come to a fork in the road, take it. One of the great things about quilting is that there are several techniques for making the same basic quilt units. I have experimented with many different techniques and have even developed techniques of my own. In this chapter, I describe the advantages and disadvantages of my preferred techniques, allowing you to choose the better fork in the road for your project.

Half-Square Triangles

A half-square triangle (HST) is a square made from two isosceles right triangles. This unit is basic to many quilt blocks and can be made in many ways.

The techniques I prefer are:
  a. The Right-Angle-Ruler technique, using a ruler designed for making HSTs such as the EZ Angle; Omnigrid® Half Square Triangle; Creative Grids Fons & Porter® Half and Quarter Ruler; or Kimberly Einmo's Easy Star & Geese Ruler by Wrights
  b. The Two-Square technique
  c. The Super-Sized Two-Square technique

Each of the patterns specifies a construction technique. If you prefer using a different technique, remember that additional fabric may be required.

Right-Angle-Ruler Technique

The advantage of the Right-Angle-Ruler technique is that half-square triangles can be made from the same width strips as the squares or rectangles used elsewhere in a block. This is my preferred technique for making HSTs from Jelly Rolls™ (2½"

wide strips) or Honey Buns™ (1½" wide strips). The disadvantage of this technique, especially when making large units, is that sewing on the bias edge may cause stretching and unit distortion.

Chart #1 (page 19) provides cut strip sizes for common sizes of HSTs.

Begin by cutting strips ½" larger than the FINISHED size of the unit. Layer two fabric strips, right sides together. Position the ruler as indicated in the manufacturer's directions. Remove the selvage and cut the first pair of triangles.

Flip the ruler and cut the second pair of triangles. Continue flipping and cutting.

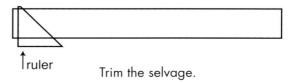

Trim the selvage.

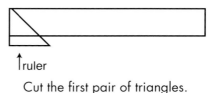

Cut the first pair of triangles.

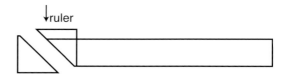

Flip the ruler and cut the second pair of triangles; flip the ruler and cut again.

Sew the triangle pairs together. Start sewing at the blunt end. Sew a scant ¼" seam. Unless otherwise indicated in the pattern, press seams toward the darker fabric. Trim the "dog ears."

Sew the pairs, press toward the
darker fabric, and trim.

Two-Square Technique

The advantage of this technique is that two units are made at the same time. Unit distortion is reduced because sewing is done before the bias edge is cut.

The precise cut size for the square is ⅞" larger than the *FINISHED* size of the unit (for example, for a finished 2" unit, cut the squares 2⅞"). I dislike cutting in ⅛" increments. The cutting instructions for patterns in the book direct you to cut squares 1" larger than the finished unit. The math is easier and the stress of "perfect" sewing is reduced.

Chart #1 (page 19) provides cut sizes for common sizes of HSTs.

Begin by cutting two squares the same size. Layer the squares right sides together.
   a. Draw a diagonal line on the wrong side of the lighter fabric square.
   b. Sew a ¼" seam on both sides of the drawn line.
   c. Cut on the drawn line.

d. Unless otherwise indicated in the pattern, press toward the darker fabric.

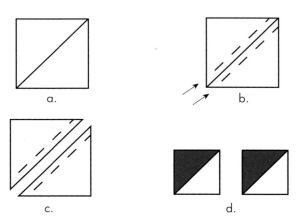

Trim the units to measure ½" larger than the finished unit size. Refer to Trimming Half-Square Triangles (page 20).

Super-Sized Two-Square Technique

The advantage of this technique is that eight identical HSTs are made at one time. This technique is particularly useful when using 5" charm squares or 10" Layer Cakes, which make 1½" and 4" finished units, respectively.

The precise cut size for the square = 2x the finished size + 1¾". Again, the cutting instructions for patterns in this book are oversized (2" is added rather than 1¾") to allow for differences in fabric thickness, sewing accuracy, and pressing. See Chart #1 (page 19) for cut sizes for common half-square triangle sizes.

Begin by cutting two squares the same size. Layer the squares right sides together.
   a. Draw two diagonal lines on the wrong side of the lighter fabric.
   b. Sew a ¼" seam on both sides of the drawn lines.
   c. Cut on both perpendiculars to make four squares.

d. Cut on the drawn lines to separate the HSTs.

e. Unless otherwise indicated in the pattern, press toward the darker fabric.

Trim the units to measure ½" larger than the finished unit size (page 20).

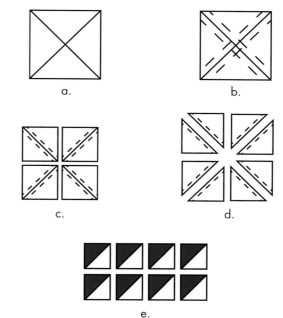

Chart #1: **Half-Square-Triangle Cutting Sizes**

Cutting sizes are slightly oversized. The HSTs are trimmed after sewing for accuracy.

Finished Unit Size	1"	1½"	2"	2½"	3"
Right-Angle-Ruler Technique (1 HST/cut)—strip width	1½"	2"	2½"	3"	3½"
Two-Square Technique (2 HSTs/square)	2" x 2"	2½" x 2½"	3" x 3"	3½" x 3½"	4" x 4"
Super-Sized Technique (8 HSTs/square)	4"	5"	6"	7"	8"

Finished Unit Size	3½"	4"	4½"	5"
Right-Angle-Ruler Technique (1 HST/cut)—strip width	4"	4½"	5"	5½"
Two-Square Technique (2 HSTs/square)	4½" x 4½"	5" x 5"	5½" x 5½"	6" x 6½"
Super-Sized Technique (8 HSTs/square)	9" x 9"	10" x 10"	11" x 11"	12" x 12"

Trimming Half-Square Triangles

To square-up HSTs, use a square ruler with a printed 45 degree (diagonal) line starting at the corner. Place the diagonal line of the ruler on the seam line with the corner of the ruler as close as possible to the corner of the unit. Trim the excess fabric from the two exposed sides.

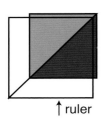 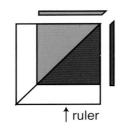

↑ruler ↑ruler

Trimming two sides of the half-square triangle unit.

Rotate the unit so that the trimmed sides are under the ruler. Align the printed diagonal line on the seam line and align the trimmed edges of the unit on the lines ½" greater than the finished size of the unit as indicated by the circles. Trim the excess from the remaining two edges.

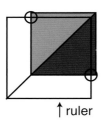 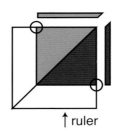

↑ruler ↑ruler

Trimming the remaining two sides.
Note: For left-handed trimming, turn both HST and ruler 90 degrees.

Flip Corners on a Rectangle Base

Flip corners are made by positioning two fabrics right sides together, sewing a diagonal seam, and pressing the flip fabric toward the corner of the base fabric. When making a single flip-

corner rectangle, either the upper-right or upper-left corner is covered by the flip corner fabric.

a. b.

Left flip corner Right flip corner

You need to determine whether you need a right-corner flip or a left-corner flip by how the unit appears in a block.
   a. Left flip corner
   b. Right flip corner
   c. Two left flip corners and two right flip corners

a. b. c.

Special names are given for rectangle units with two flip corners. Flip corners on the same long side of a rectangle base result in a flying geese unit. Flip corners on two opposite corners of the rectangle base result in a parallelogram, with either left-corner or right-corner flips. Directions for these units are given later in this chapter (pages 24 & 26).

Flying geese Parallelogram

Flip-Corner Square (*FCS*) Technique

The advantage of the Flip-Corner Square (**FCS**) technique is that both the rectangle bases and the flip-corner squares are cut from the same width strips. This technique is great for patterns calling for Jelly Roll or Honey Bun strips. I prefer this for making multi-fabric units or when I'm working with precut fabric strips.

In this technique, the rectangle base is cut ½" larger than the finished dimensions of the unit. The flip-corner square is cut ½" larger than the finished width of the unit. Chart #2 (page 23) provides cut sizes for common size units.

Begin by cutting a rectangle base and a flip-corner square.

    a. Draw a diagonal line on the wrong side of the flip-corner square.

    b. For a left-corner flip, position the square so the drawn line goes from the lower-left side to upper-right corner of the rectangle base.

    c. For a right-corner flip, position the square so the drawn line goes from the lower-right side to the upper-left corner of the rectangle base.

    d. Sew from the long side of the rectangle base to the corner on the drawn line. Press the flip corner toward the corner.

After pressing, you have three options for dealing with the extra fabric layers.

Option 1: Leave all the layers in place.

Option 2: Remove only the center layer (the underside of the **FCS**).

Option 3: Remove center and rectangle base layers.

Option 4: Make "waste not want not" half-square triangles from the excess center and rectangle base layers.

In Options 1 and 2, leaving the rectangle base intact keeps the unit square. If the flip corner is slightly off, the rectangle base will serve as a guide for further piecing. Option 3 eliminates bulk and is often the preferred technique for hand quilters.

For Option 4:

    a. After sewing on the drawn line and before pressing, sew another seam ½" from the first.

    b. Cut between the two lines of stitching (as indicated by the blue line). Press.

    c. The result is a trimmed flip-corner rectangle and a half-square triangle.

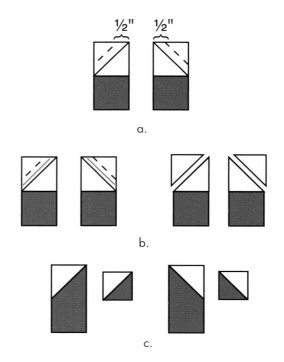

a.

    a.   b.   c.

d.

Left flip-corner rectangle   Right flip-corner rectangle

Flip-Corner-Triangle (*FCT*) Technique

I developed a Flip-Corner-Triangle (*FCT*) technique for making flip-corner units.

The advantage of this technique is that it requires less fabric and eliminates trimming the center layer. Proper positioning of the triangle may take a little practice, but once mastered your piecing will be quicker.

As before, cut the rectangle base ½" larger than the finished dimensions.

To make the *FCT*, cut a square 1" larger than the FINISHED WIDTH of the unit. Cut the square once on the diagonal. (The triangles are oversized to allow for squaring-up the unit after sewing.)

From template plastic or cardboard, cut a square ½" larger than the FINISHED WIDTH of the unit. Cut the square once on the diagonal to make a marking template. Use the template to draw a sewing line on the wrong side of the rectangle base. Chart #2 provides cut sizes for common sizes of these units.

Using the rectangle base, *FCT*, and template:
   a. For a left-corner flip, place the template over the RIGHT corner of the WRONG side of the rectangle base. Draw a line along the template.
   b. For a right-corner flip, place the template over the LEFT corner of the WRONG side of the rectangle base. Draw a line along the template.

Template placement for a left flip   Template placement for a right flip

The position may seem counter intuitive—just remember you will be sewing on the wrong side of the base fabric.

With right sides together, position the flip triangle on the RIGHT side of the rectangle base with the hypotenuse (long side) of the triangle in the same direction as the drawn line and the edge extending a scant ¼" toward the corner beyond the line.

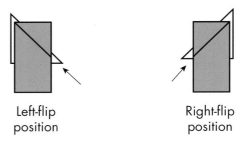

Left-flip position   Right-flip position

Sew on the drawn line, beginning on the long side of the rectangle base and continue sewing toward the corner. Press the seam toward the corner.

Measure the unit. The correct size is ½" larger than the finished unit size. If the triangle does not cover the rectangle base, you've positioned the triangle too far above the line. If the triangle extends beyond the rectangle base, refer to Trimming Flip-Corner Units (page 28).

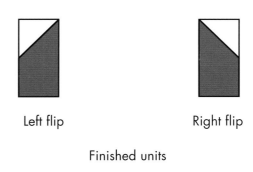

Left flip   Right flip

Finished units

Flip-Corner-Split Rectangles

Many blocks contain half-square triangles joined to a square. Another way to look at this unit is as a flip-corner split rectangle.

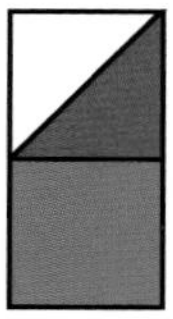

Left flip-corner
split rectangle

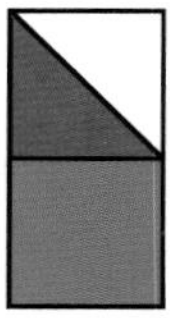

Right flip-corner
split rectangle

Begin by making a strip-set from two strips cut half the finished unit length plus ½". Press toward the darker fabric unless otherwise indicated in the pattern. Cut rectangle bases the same width as the cut dimension of the strips. Add the flip

corner using either the Flip-Corner Square or Flip-Corner Triangle technique (pages 21 & 22).

By adding a second flip corner to the flip-corner rectangles you can make either split parallelograms or split flying geese.

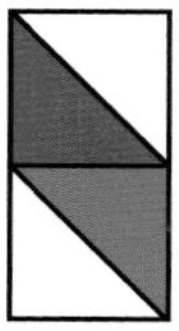

Right flip-
corner split
parallelogram

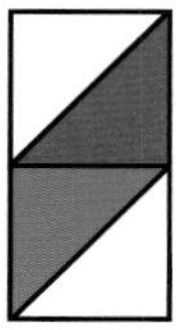

Left flip-
corner split
parallelogram

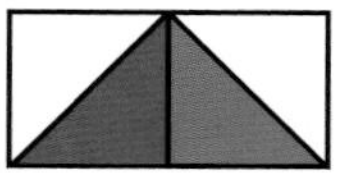

Split flying
geese

Chart #2: Cut Sizes for Flip Corners on a Rectangle Base

Finished Size	1" x 2"	1½" x 3"	2" x 4"	2½" x 5"	3" x 6"	3½" x 7"	4" x 8"
Rectangle Base (1/unit)	1½" x 2½"	2" x 3½"	2½" x 4½"	3" x 5½"	3½" x 6½"	4" x 7½"	4½" x 8½"
Split Base (strip width)	1½"	2"	2½"	3"	3½"	4"	4½"
Flip-Corner Square	1½" x 1½"	2" x 2"	2½" x 2½"	3" x 3"	3½" x 3½"	4" x 4"	4½" x 4½"
Flip-Corner Triangle*	2" x 2"	2½" x 2½"	3" x 3"	3½" x 3½"	4" x 4"	4½" x 4½"	5" x 5"
Template Size*	1½" x 1½"	2" x 2"	2½" x 2½"	3" x 3"	3½" x 3½"	4" x 4"	4½" x 4½"

*The flip-corner triangle and template are made by cutting the square once on the diagonal.

Flying Geese

Flying geese are composed of a center isosceles right triangle with smaller isosceles right triangles sewn to each side.

I once took a class where we made flying geese. The next day the teacher said we were going to make star points. I couldn't see the difference between the two units. In my world, if it looks like a goose and is sewn like a goose, it's a goose.

A classmate later tried to explain the difference—something about color placement or the direction of the wings in the finished block. I'll just refer to these units as flying geese and leave it to you to determine the difference.

Traditionally, flying geese are made from three triangles. Deg Tucker's Studio 180 Design uses four small squares and one large square to make four flying geese at once. Both Deb's Tucker Trimmer and Eleanor Burns's specialty rulers are designed to trim common sizes of flying geese.

However, you only need a rectangular ruler with 45-degree lines intersecting ¼" from the edge.

I prefer the Two-Square and Flip-Corner techniques for making flying geese.

Two-Square Technique

Begin by cutting a square 1½" larger than the finished length of the unit for the goose body (the center triangle). Cut a second square from a different fabric 3" larger than the finished length of the unit for the wings (the side triangles). Refer to Chart #3 (page 25) for cut sizes for common size units.

a.

Draw a diagonal line on the wrong side of the smaller square.

b.

With right sides together, position the smaller square in the center of the larger square.

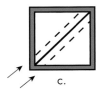

c.

Sew ¼" on both sides of the drawn line. Cut on the drawn line.

d.

Press the seam allowances toward the larger triangles.

e.

With right sides together, position the two squares so that opposite fabrics touch, aligning the outside edges.

f.

Draw a diagonal line across the seams.

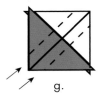

g.

Sew ¼" on both sides of the drawn line. Cut on the drawn line.

h.

Clip the seam allowance midway between the horizontal seams so you can press the seam allowances toward the larger triangles.

To trim the units:

↑ruler

a. Position the ruler with the ¼" line at the top point of the center triangle and the 45-degree lines on the seams. Cut along the top. Repeat this for other half.

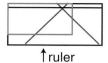

↑ruler

b. Mark the cut (unfinished) size of the unit on the ruler using tape or grease pencil (shown in green).

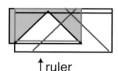
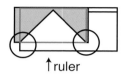

↑ruler   ↑ruler

c. Position the ruler so the top cut edge is aligned with the edge of the ruler and the bottom points align with the marked lines on the ruler.

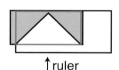
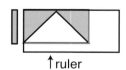

↑ruler   ↑ruler

d. Trim the left side.

↑ruler

e. Rotate the unit. Reposition the ruler with the lines on the top and side of the unit. Trim the bottom and other side.

f. Repeat to trim the remaining unit.

To make units with dark bodies and light wings, cut the smaller square from a dark fabric and the larger square from a light fabric.

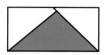

Flying geese variation

This technique can also be used to make random flying geese. Cut the squares from a variety of light and dark fabrics—either light bodies (small square) and dark wings (large square) or dark bodies (small square) and light wings (large square).

After the first sewing, pair different units. The results will be flying geese with two different wings.

Random flying geese

This is not the method to use if you want four identical units with (for example) red left wings and blue right wings. Using two sets of squares with the same body fabric (the small square) and two different wing fabrics (the red and blue large squares) results in mirror-image units—two with red left wings and two with red right wings.

Chart #3: Cut Sizes for Flying Geese

Two-Square Technique (4 units/square set)

Finished Size	1" x 2"	1½" x 3"	2" x 4"	2½" x 5"
For the Center Triangle	3½" x 3½"	4½" x 4½"	5½" x 5½"	6½" x 6½"
For the Side Triangles	5" x 5"	6" x 6"	7" x 7"	8" x 8"

Two-Square Technique (continued)

Finished Size	3" x 6"	3½" x 7"	4" x 8"
For the Center Triangle	7½" x 7½"	8½" x 8½"	9½" x 9½"
For the Side Triangles	9" x 9"	10" x 10"	11" x 11"

Chart #3: Cut Sizes for Flying Geese (continued)

Flip-Corner Technique

Finished Size	1" x 2"	1½" x 3"	2" x 4"	2½" x 5"
Rectangle Base (center triangle)	1½" x 2"	2" x 3½"	2½" x 4½"	3" x 5½"
Flip-Corner Square (side triangles)	1½" x 1½"	2" x 2"	2½" x 2½"	3" x 3"
OR				
Flip-Corner Triangle (1/unit)*	2" x 2"	½" x 2½"	3" x 3"	3½" x 3½"
Template Size*	1½" x 1½"	2" x 2"	2½" x 2½"	3" x 3"

Flip-Corner Technique (continued)

Finished Size	3" x 6"	3½" x 7"	4" x 8"
Rectangle Base (center triangle)	3½" x 6½"	4" x 7½"	4½" x 8½"
Flip-Corner Square (side triangles)	3½" x 3½"	4" x 4"	4½" x 4½"
OR			
Flip-Corner Triangle (1/unit)*	4" x 4"	4½" x 4½"	5" x 5"
Template Size*	3½" x 3½"	4" x 4"	4½" x 4½"

*Flip triangles and templates are made by cutting the squares once on the diagonal.

Parallelograms

Think of a parallelogram as a flying goose with a broken wing. In flying geese units, the flip corners are on two adjacent corners of the long side of the rectangle base. In a parallelogram, two opposite corners of the rectangle base are flipped.

This unit can be made in two different directions. For a left parallelogram, flip toward the upper-left and lower-right corners. For a right parallelogram, flip toward the upper-right and lower-left corners.

It is important to pay attention to the direction of the slant in the pattern instructions.

Left parallelogram

Right parallelogram

Parallelograms can be made using **FCS**s or **FCT**s.

The rectangle base is cut ½" larger than the finished dimensions of the unit.

A **FCS** is cut ½" larger than the finished width of the unit.

A **FCS** begins with a square cut 1" larger than the finished width of the unit, then cut once on the diagonal. The template square is cut ½" larger than the finished width of the unit, then cut once on the diagonal. Chart # 2 (page 23) provides cut sizes for common size units.

Follow the directions for a flip-corner rectangle, then add the second flip corner at the opposite corner of the rectangle base.

Cut sizes for parallelograms are the same as for flying geese. See Chart #3.

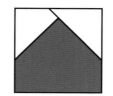
Adjacent flip corners

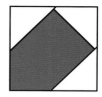
Three flip corners

When all four corners on a square base are flipped, the unit is called a square-in-a-square. Traditionally, this unit is made from a center square surrounded by four isosceles right triangles. The same results can be achieved by flipping all four corners on a square base. This technique is easier to cut and construct than the traditional method.

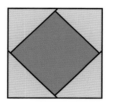
Square-in-a-square
(four flip corners)

Flip Corners on a Square Base

If you can flip corners on a rectangle base, flipping one or more corners on a square base is as easy as pie. Units with a single corner, two opposite corners, two adjacent corners, and three corners are excellent replacement units.

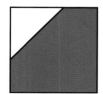
Single flip corner

Opposite flip corners

For each unit, cut a base square and EITHER **FCS**s OR **FCT**s. Cut the base square ½" larger than the finished size of the unit. Cut flip-corner squares half the finished size of the unit + ½". For a flip-corner triangle, begin with a square half the finished size of the unit + 1", then cut once on the diagonal. Chart #4 provides cut sizes for common unit sizes (page 28).

Chart #4: Cut Sizes for Flip Corners on a Square Base

Flip Corners on a Square Base (square in-a-square)

Finished Size	2" x 2"	3" x 3"	4" x 4"	5" x 5"	6" x 6"
Base Square (1/unit)	2½" x 2½"	3½" x 3½"	4½" x 4½"	5½" x 5½"	6½" x 6½"
Flip-Corner Square (cut 4)	1½" x 1½"	2" x 2"	2½" x 2½"	3" x 3"	3½" x 3½"
OR					
Flip-Corner Triangle*	2" x 2"	2½" x 2½"	3" x 3"	3½" x 3½"	4" x 4"
Template Size*	1½" x 1½"	2" x 2"	2½" x 2½"	3" x 3"	3½" x 3½"

*Flip-corner triangles and templates are made by cutting the squares once on the diagonal.

Flip Corners on a Square Base (continued)

Finished Size	7" x 7"	8" x 8"	9" x 9"	10" x 10"	12" x 12"
Base Square (1/unit)	7½" x 7½"	8½" x 8½"	9½" x 9½"	10½" x 10½"	12½" x 12½"
Flip-Corner Square (cut 4)	4" x 4"	4½" x 4½"	5" x 5"	5½" x 5½"	6" x 6"
OR					
Flip-Corner Triangle*	4½" x 4½"	5" x 5"	5½" x 5½"	6" x 6"	6½" x 6½"
Template Size*	4" x 4"	4½" x 4½"	5" x 5"	5½" x 5½"	6" x 6"

*Flip-corner triangles and templates are made by cutting the squares once on the diagonal.

Trimming Flip-Corner Units

If the corner of the base square is not covered by the flip fabric, the problem is caused by improper cutting, positioning, or sewing of the flip-corner fabric. Check that the flip-corner piece is the correct size and that sewing lines are correctly drawn. Sew on the edge of the drawn line closest to the corner instead of down the center of the line.

Flip corner doesn't cover the base

More likely, the flip-corner fabric will extend beyond the edges of the base fabric. Improper pressing may also cause misshapen units. The urge to slide the iron across the seam toward the corner is strong, and generally results in stretching the flip-corner fabric.

Flip corner extends beyond the base

Whatever the cause, when the flip-corner fabric extends beyond the base fabric, the unit will need to be squared-up.

Place the unit on the cutting mat with the wrong side of the base fabric facing up. Position the ruler lines indicating the desired size of the unit on the edges of the base fabric. Trim excess fabric from the two exposed edges. If necessary, repeat the process for any other flipped corners on the unit.

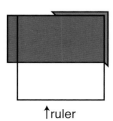 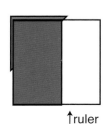

↑ruler   ↑ruler

Trimming a right   Trimming a left
flip corner   flip corner

Quarter-Square-Triangle/Hourglass Units

A quarter-square triangle is made by combining four triangles into a square. When the opposite quarter squares are the same fabric, the unit is called an hourglass.

Traditional construction of an hourglass unit

I dislike cutting individual triangles and sewing cut bias edges together. An easier and quicker way to make this unit is to combine two half-square triangle units. Sewing squares to make triangles is a nice way to avoid sewing cut bias edges.

Squares for this unit should be 1¼" larger than the finished unit size. However, cutting the squares 1½" larger than the finished unit takes the stress out of sewing. Squaring-up the unit ensures accuracy. Refer to Chart #5 (page 31) for cut sizes for common unit sizes.

Begin by cutting two squares.

a. Draw two diagonal lines on the wrong side of the lighter fabric.

b. With right sides together, sew a ¼" seam on both sides of ONE of the drawn lines.

c. Cut on the drawn line to make two half-square triangles. Unless otherwise indicated in the pattern, press the seam allowances toward the darker fabric.

d. Extend the diagonal line onto the dark fabric on the wrong side of one of the HSTs.

e. With right sides of the contrasting triangles together and the raw edges aligned, sew a ¼" seam on both sides of the drawn line.

f. Cut on the diagonal line.

g. Clip the seam allowances and press in opposite directions.

h. The result is two hourglass units.

Trimming Hourglass Units

The cutting sizes given in the patterns in this book are oversized. It will be necessary to trim the hourglass unit to size.

After pressing the unit, position the diagonal line of a square ruler on one of the diagonal seams. Slide the ruler along the diagonal seam until the other diagonal seam aligns with the marks on the ruler ½" larger than the finished size of the unit. Trim excess fabric from the two exposed sides.

Turn the unit 180 degrees and trim the remaining two sides. Note: For left-handed trimming, place the ruler on the corners opposite of those shown.

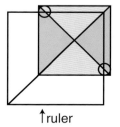 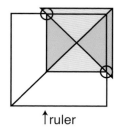

↑ruler   ↑ruler

Trimming the hourglass unit

Chart #5: Cut Sizes for Quarter-Square-Triangle/Hourglass Units

Quarter-Square-Triangle/Hourglass Units

Finished Size	2" x 2"	2½" x 2½"	3" x 3"	3½" x 3½"	4" x 4"
Cut 1 square from each of two fabrics (to the precise size).	3¼" x 3¼"	3¾" x 3¾"	4¼" x 4¼"	4¾" x 4¾"	5¼" x 5¼"
OR					
Cut 1 square from each of two fabrics (oversized).	3½" x 3½"	4" x 4"	4½" x 4½"	5" x 5"	5½" x 5½"

Quarter-Square-Triangle/Hourglass Units (continued)

Finished Size	4½" x 4½"	5" x 5"	5½" x 5½"	6" x 6"
Cut 1 square from each of two fabrics (to the precise size).	5¾" x 5¾"	6¼" x 6¼"	6 ¾" x 6¾"	7¼" x 7¼"
OR				
Cut 1 square from each of two fabrics (oversized).	6" x 6"	6½" x 6½"	7" x 7"	7½" x 7½"

◆ General Information

Fabric

Fabric is one of the most important factors in making a successful quilt. Purchase 100-percent cotton fabric of the best quality you can afford. Many manufacturers print the same design on different quality fabrics (known as greige goods). Learning to feel the fabric's quality is an important and quickly acquired skill. Learn to use the feel of the fabric, not the price, to determine fabric quality.

I've sewn with both poor and high quality fabric. The latter is my preference. Construction is easier, the final product looks better, and the quilt will last longer. I do often let the type of project determine the fabric quality. I don't see the need to spend "big bucks" on fabric for a seasonal wallhanging I'll never wash.

Once you've purchased the fabric, as Hamlet (if he were a quilter) would ask, "To prewash or not to prewash? That is the question." Prewashing is a matter of personal preference. If the fabric might bleed or shrink excessively, prewashing is a good idea.

Running hot water over the fabric will immediately let you know if the fabric will bleed. Prewash the fabric the same way you plan to wash the finished quilt. Laundry detergents tend to remove the fabric preservatives, something to keep in mind if you are planning on stashing the fabric. Many laundry detergents have scents or softeners. I prefer to use Orvus® soap, which has no additives.

I put several muslin squares or commercial color catchers in the wash to absorb any discharged color. The dryer will take care of shrinkage.

Mixing prewashed and unwashed fabrics in the same project may result in uneven shrinkage when the final project is washed. If you prewash the fabric used in the quilt top, prewash the backing fabric.

Prewashing often results in raveled edges. On yardage, snipping a triangle off each corner may prevent raveling and fraying during the wash cycle. Smaller pieces can be washed in a mesh lingerie bag. I avoid prewashing fat quarters and fat eighths in a machine. They can shrink or distort from the machine agitation, the result being not large enough to produce the required number of pieces. I prewash smaller fabric cuts with a soak and a swish in the sink.

With all that said, I seldom feel the need to prewash. I'm usually so excited to start a new project that I don't want to spend the time washing and ironing fabric. I'll leave the prewashing decision to you.

Cathy Busch ◈ Newfangled Piecing: Faster & Easier

Rotary Cutter

Rotary cutters have become a quilter's best friend. Unfortunately, the cutting edge of the blade is too often overlooked. A sharp blade will make cutting easier and more accurate. Accurate cutting will help ensure that the block pieces fit together properly. Many quilters buy expensive fabric and then try to cut it with a dull or nicked blade. Cutting corners by not changing the rotary blade often results in badly cut pieces.

Checking Seam Allowance

Take the time to check your seam allowance before beginning to sew pieces together. Even if you have a ¼" foot designed for your machine, the thickness of fabric, the thread, and even the type of needle used can affect piecing.

To check your seam allowance cut 3 strips 2½" x 6½" from the project fabric.

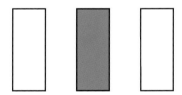

Sew the longs sides together and press toward the center strip. The center strip should measure 2" and the block should measure 6½" x 6½".

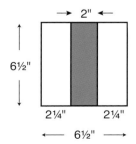

If the measurements are not correct, try again with wider or narrower seams until the measurements are correct. This may involve moving the needle position, changing the weight of the thread, or changing the size of the needle.

Pressing

Careful pressing is just as important as cutting and sewing accurately. Paraphrasing Yogi Berra, "Ninety percent of quilting is sewing, the other half is pressing." The objective of pressing is to get the piecework to lie flat without stretching. Use an up-and-down pressing motion rather than a side-to-side sliding motion with the iron. Seams are generally pressed toward the darker fabric unless otherwise indicated in the pattern.

Begin by positioning the pieces on the ironing surface with the darker fabric on top and the seam allowance away from you. Using an up-and-down motion, move the iron the length of the seam to set the seam.

Lift the darker fabric (so that you are pressing on the right side of the fabric) and press the seam away from you. I find that pressing on the wrong side of the fabric often results in humps, bumps, and sometimes pleats. Remember, the right side of the project is the side that you want to lie smooth and flat.

Split Pressing Seams

Splitting the seam allowance is a helpful way to reduce bulk and keep piecework flat. Use this technique when two seams intersect, as at the center of a four-patch unit. Use a seam ripper or pin and "unsew" (remove) the stitches that are in the seam allowance. Finger press the seams in opposite directions. Press the seams flat.

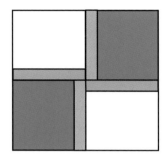

Straightening Quilt Edges

A quilt top with blocks set on point often needs to be straightened before adding borders or binding because most patterns have slightly oversized setting triangles. Place the ¼" line of a rotary ruler on the setting triangle intersections. Trim the excess fabric. Repeat the process around the perimeter of the quilt.

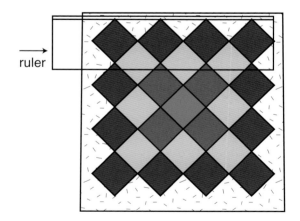

ruler

Straight Borders

When the blocks are made and sewn together, take your time cutting and attaching the borders. A straight border is made from a single fabric cut from the length or width of fabric. (Pieced borders are made from consistent or randomly sized pieces of fabric or from pieced units or blocks.)

For wide borders on larger quilts, I like to cut my borders from the length of the fabric. I buy yardage equal to the longest unbordered side. This provides me enough fabric for borders, binding, and often a hanging sleeve.

Many of the quilts in this book include a skinny inner border (SIB). Consider the center of your quilt as a work of art. The SIB is the mat board that separates the art from the frame. When the SIB matches the background fabric, it is sometimes referred to as a "floating border." I like to use a floating border when the final border fabric is busy.

An SIB from a fabric other than the block background fabric acts as a fence, separating the blocks from the final border fabric. Black is a good color for a SIB fence. Alternatively, select a fabric that serves as a transition from the colors in the blocks to the colors in the outer-border fabric.

Finished quilt tops may have slightly irregular dimensions. When adding a straight border, measure the length of the quilt top in three places—down the center and along the two sides. Add the three numbers together and divide by three to determine the length of the side borders.

Measuring Tape

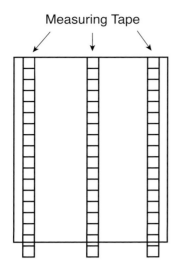

When joining border strips, use a 45-degree angle seam except for striped fabrics, which should be joined with straight seams. Press the seams open.

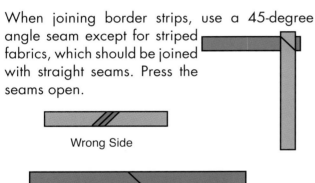

Wrong Side

Right Side

To ensure the borders are the same length, fold the border strip in half across the width, then cut the both borders at the same time.

When adding the borders to the quilt top, fold each border in half, then in fourths, marking the folds with pins. Similarly, fold the quilt top in half and then in fourths, marking these points with pins. With right sides together, pin the borders to the quilt, matching the pins to even out and ease slight irregularities in the quilt dimensions.

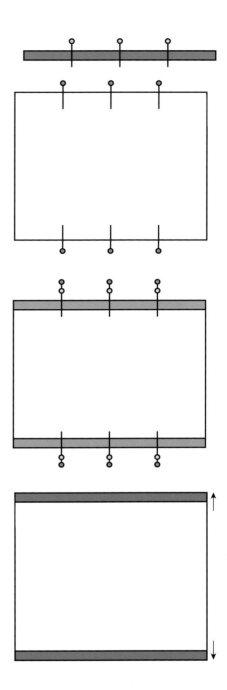

Use a walking foot to attach the borders. If the quilt top and the borders are the same length, sew with the border on top. If there is extra fullness in either the top or the border, sew with the longer piece on the bottom. This will let the feed dogs ease in any fullness. Unless otherwise indicated, press the seams toward the borders.

Repeat the process for the top and bottom borders, taking three measurements across the width of the quilt top including the side borders, then average them.

Follow the same procedure when attaching outer borders.

Quilt Backing

You've spent time and money making your quilt top. Doesn't the back deserve equal attention? Do you want the back to coordinate with the front? Do you want to use up that "bargain" fabric you bought years ago? Do you have extra blocks you want to incorporate into the back? Do you just want the project to be done?

Consider the quilting design, style, and method when selecting backing fabric. Quilting is much more visible on a plain, solid color fabric than on a printed fabric. The number of seams in a highly pieced back will increase the bulk of the project.

Treat the quilt back as you treated the quilt top. If the fabrics in the top are prewashed, do the same for the backing fabric. I hate to admit that I sometimes find the back more interesting than the quilt top.

The quilt backing needs to be larger than the top to provide fabric for loading the quilt onto a frame or a longarm machine and the shrinkage that occurs as it is quilted. Hand quilters find a back 4"–6" larger than the quilt top is sufficient. Machine quilters often require the back to be 6"–8" larger than the top.

Binding

For straight edged quilts, I recommend using French or a double binding cut on the straight-of-grain. Curved edge quilts require a bias binding. Depending on the thickness of the batting, I cut the binding strips 2"–2½" wide. The patterns in this book allow for 2½" wide binding strips.

Square-up the quilt before adding the binding. Using a long rectangular ruler, measure out from the border seam and trim to a consistent width. Reposition the ruler and continue trimming around the quilt.

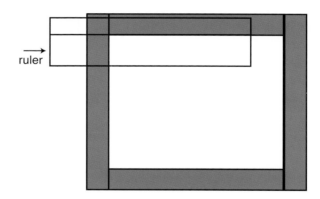

ruler

Measure the perimeter of the quilt and add 10" to allow for mitering the corners and joining the ends of the binding together.

Example – Quilt top 52" x 68"
52" + 52" + 68" + 68" + 10" = 250"
250" ÷ 40" = 6.25 or 7 width-of-fabric strips

Join strips using a 45-degree angle seam. Press the seams open. Press a 45-degree angle on one end of the binding. Then press the binding in half lengthwise, wrong sides together.

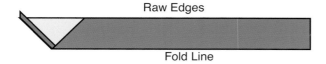

Raw Edges

Fold Line

To begin, position the 45-degree angle end of the binding 6"–8" away from the corner on the bottom edge of the quilt. Lay the binding around the quilt to check that the seams in the binding do not end up on the quilt's corners. Adjust the starting position if necessary.

Attach the binding to the quilt using a walking foot. This foot prevents puckering when sewing through all the layers. Match the raw edges of the binding to the right side of the quilt. Start stitching 4"–8" from the end of the binding.

Sew to within ¼" of the corner. Stitch a 45-degree seam toward the corner of the quilt. Lift the needle and cut the thread.

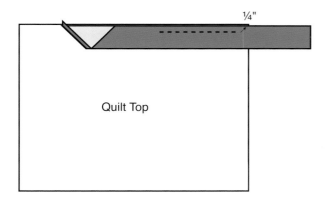

¼"

Quilt Top

Fold the binding away from the quilt along the 45-degree stitching line. Then fold the binding straight down onto itself. Match the raw edges of the binding and the quilt. Begin sewing from the edge to create a mitered corner.

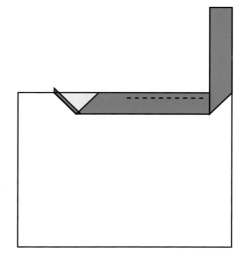

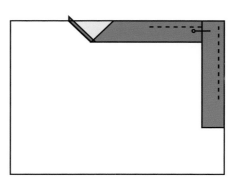

Continue sewing, repeating corner instructions until about 10" from the first edge of the binding. Insert the binding into the open end. Trim the end of the binding and pin it in place. Continue sewing until the binding is completely attached. Hand-stitch the join.

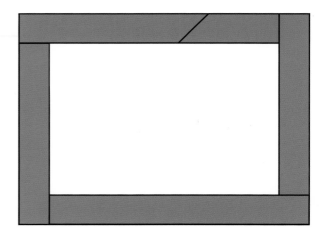

Bring the folded edge of the binding to the back side of the quilt so that it covers the stitching. The miter on the right side is formed by folding the binding to the back side.

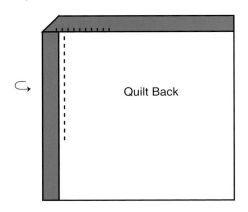

Quilt Back

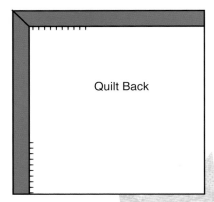

Quilt Back

Naming Your Quilt and Attaching the Label

"It ain't over 'til it's over," as Yogi Berra famously said. Two things are left to do. First, you need a title for your quilt. It's common to name it after the name of the pattern design used. I prefer to pick my own names for my quilts.

Many of my quilts are named for the people who inspired or helped me in the quilt making process. When I look at the quilt, I am reminded of their kindness. Unfortunately, it's now to the point where my friends are afraid to help, lest their name shows in the title.

I also name quilts for the experience that began the process. TURNING TWENTY is a great name, but my quilt is titled TWO HUNDRED MILES, FIVE QUILT SHOPS, ROAD TRIP WITH FRIENDS. Whenever I look at the quilt I remember that day.

The way I set the blocks in the quilt has often been incorporated into the title. TRIP TO … or WHAT'S THE POINT OF … remind me how I made the quilt.

On occasion, I have a great name and then make the quilt. Consider DO NOT GO GENTLE INTO THAT GOOD NIGHT. I see this quilt made from Kaffe Fassett or Amanda Bloom bright fabrics, full of stars and sharp angles. Now all I need is a nephew named Dylan or a poetry lover to receive the quilt.

The last thing to do is sign your work. Take the time to make a label with the title, your name, the quilter's name (if other than you), the year you started or completed, and any other information you want to identify your quilt. If I am having the quilt machine quilted, I attach my label to the quilt backing first. Then I don't have to do any hand sewing and the label is permanently affixed to the quilt.

Labels are important to you and those who receive the quilt. After my mother-in-law passed away, we found several unsigned embroidered quilts in the closet. I knew she hadn't made the quilts. I'll never know who made them or when they were made. Don't let your work join the thousands of unknown quilts.

AFTER APRIL'S SNOW

AFTER APRIL'S SNOW, 53" x 65", made by the author, quilted by Julie Messerly, Cedar Falls, Iowa

Finished Block Size—12" x 12"

Long winters can be depressing. I made this tribute to spring to brighten my home and spirit. Hourglass and flying geese units make the quilt center a snap. The Super-Sized technique for half-square triangles speeds the Pinwheel block construction.

Yardage

Pink floral–⅜ yard (Star block centers)
Green–1 yard (Star block points)
Yellow background–1 yard
Blue-and-yellow print–½ yard (hourglass units)
Light background–⅜ yard (hourglass units)
Green–⅞ yard (first and third borders)
Pink print–¾ yard (Pinwheel blocks)
Yellow print–¾ yard (Pinwheel blocks)
Blue-and-white print (square-in-a-square corners)–

> ½ yard (if using the Flip-Corner Triangle technique)
> OR
> ¾ yard (if using the Flip-Corner Square technique)

White floral print–⅝ yard
Binding–½ yard
Backing–4¼ yards
Batting–61" x 73"

Cutting Instructions

From the pink floral fabric:
- Cut 1 strip 4½" wide. Cut into 6 squares 4½" x 4½" (large Star block centers).
- Cut 2 strips 3½" wide. Cut into 18 squares 3½" x 3½" (border Star block centers).

From the green fabric:
- Cut 2 strips 7" wide. Cut into 6 squares 7" x 7" (Star block flying geese units) and

- Substitute any six 12" blocks for the quilt center.

- Make the quilt smaller by eliminating the pieced and/or solid border.

- Make the quilt larger with an additional solid border.

5 squares 6" x 6" (border Star block flying geese units).
- Cut 3 strips 6" wide. Cut into 18 squares 6" x 6" (border flying geese wings).

From the yellow background fabric:
- Cut 1 strip 5½" wide. Cut into 6 squares 5½" x 5½" (large flying geese center triangles).
- Cut 2 strips 2½" wide. Cut into 24 squares 2½"x 2½" (large Star block corners).
- Cut 3 strips 4½" wide. Cut into 18 squares 4½" x 4½" (border flying geese center triangles).
- Cut 4 strips 2" wide. Cut into 72 squares 2" x 2" (border Star block corners).

From the blue-and-yellow print:
- Cut 2 strips 5½" wide. Cut into 12 squares 5½" x 5½" (hourglass and flying geese center triangles).
- Cut 1 strip 4½" wide. Cut into 2 squares 4½" x 4½" and 6 rectangles 4½" x 2½". Trim the remaining strip to 2½" wide and cut 4 squares 2½"x 2½".

From the light background fabric:
- Cut 1 strip 5½" wide. Cut into 7 squares 5½" x 5½" (hourglass units).
- Cut 1 strip 7" wide. Cut into 5 squares 7" x 7" (flying geese wings).

From the pink print:
- Cut 4 strips 6" wide. Cut into 19 squares 6" x 6" (border Pinwheel blocks).

From the yellow print:
- Cut 4 strips 6" wide. Cut into 19 squares 6" x 6" (border Pinwheel blocks).

From the green border fabric:
- Cut 4 strips 2½" wide (first border).
- Cut 5 strips 3½" wide (third border).

From the white floral print:
- Cut 3 strips 6½" wide. Cut into 18 squares 6½" x 6½"(square-in-a-square centers).

From the blue-and-white print:
- For flip-corner triangles, cut 4 strips 4" wide. Cut into 36 squares 4" x 4". Cut each square once on the diagonal to make 72 **FCT**s. Cut a 3½" x 3½" square from cardboard or template plastic. Cut once on the diagonal to make a marking template.

OR
- For flip-corner squares, cut 7 strips 3½" wide. Cut into 72 **FCS**s 3½" x 3½".

From the binding fabric:
- Cut 6 strips 2½" wide.

Sewing Instructions

1. Using the Two-Square technique (page 18), make 24 flying geese units from 6 green 7" x 7" squares and 6 yellow background 5½" x 5½" squares. The units should measure 2½" x 4½".

Make 24.

2. Sew 2 flying geese from Step 1 to both sides of pink floral 4½" x 4½" squares. Press the seams toward the center square. Make 6. The units should measure 4½" x 8½".

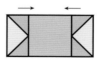

Make 6.

3. Sew yellow background 2½" x 2½" squares to both sides of the remaining 12 flying geese. Press toward the corner squares. The units should measure 2½" x 8½".

Make 12.

4. Join 2 units from Step 3 to the top and bottom of the units from Step 2 to complete the Star blocks. Press the seams toward the center row. Make 6. The units should measure 8½" x 8½".

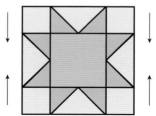

Make 6 Star blocks.

5. Make 14 hourglass units (pages 29–30) from 7 blue-and-yellow print 5½" x 5½" squares and 7 light background 5½" x 5½" squares. Split-press (page 34) the center seams. Trim the units (page 30) to 4½" x 4½".

Make 14.

6. Join 2 units from Step 5 to make 7 hourglass pairs. Press the seams open. The units should measure 4½" x 8½".

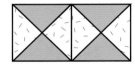

Make 7 hourglass pairs.

7. Using the Two-Square technique, make 20 flying geese from 5 light background 7" x 7" squares and 5 blue-and-yellow print 5½" x 5½" squares. The units should measure 2½" x 4½".

Make 20.

8. Join 2 units from Step 7 to make 10 flying geese pairs. Press the seams open. The units should measure 2½" x 8½".

Make 10 flying geese pairs.

Quilt Assembly

1. Arrange the Star blocks, flying geese pairs, hourglass pairs, blue-and-yellow print 2½" x 2½" squares, 2½" x 4½" rectangles, and 4½" x 4½" squares in rows as shown in the row assembly diagram. Join the units into rows and sew the rows together, pressing the seams as indicated. The center should measures 24½" x 36½".

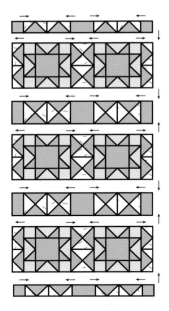

Row assembly

2. Cut the side borders from the green 2½" first-border strips 36½" long and add to the sides (pages 34–36). Cut the top and bottom borders 28½" long and add to the quilt. Press the seams toward the border. For the pieced border to fit, the quilt top must measure 28½" x 40½".

3. Using the Super-Sized-Square technique (page 18), make 152 HSTs from 19 pink print 6" x 6" squares and 19 yellow print 6" x 6" squares. Trim the units to 2½" x 2½" (page 20).

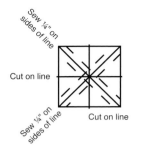

Make 152.

4. Sew 4 HSTs from Step 11 to make a Pinwheel block. Split-press the center seams. Make 38. The units should measure 4½" x 4½".

Make 38 Pinwheel blocks.

5. Refer to the quilt assembly diagram (page 44) and join 10 Pinwheel blocks to make the side borders. Press the seams in one direction. The borders should measure 4½" x 40½". Add to the sides of the quilt. Press the seams toward the green border.

6. Join 9 Pinwheel blocks to make the top and bottom borders. Press the seams in one direction. The borders should measure 4½" x 36½". Add to the quilt. Press the seams toward the green border. The quilt should measure 36½" x 48½".

7. Join 5 green 3½" third-border strips end-to-end. Cut 2 side borders 48½" long. Add to the quilt. Cut 2 borders 42½" long. Add to the top and bottom of the quilt. Press the seams toward the second green border. The quilt should measure 42½" x 54½".

8. Make 18 square-in-a-square units (page 27) from 18 white floral print 6½" x 6½" squares and EITHER 72 blue-and-white **FCT**s OR 3½" x 3½" **FCS**s. The units should measure 6½" x 6½".

Make 18.

9. Using the Two-Square technique, make 72 flying geese from 18 green 6" x 6" squares and 18 yellow background 4½" x 4½" squares. The units should measure 2" x 3½".

Make 72.

10. Sew flying geese from Step 16 to both sides of a center pink floral 3½" x 3½" square. Press the seams toward the center square. Make 18. The units should measure 2" x 6½".

Make 18.

11. Sew yellow background 2" x 2" squares to both sides of the remaining 36 flying geese units. Press the seams toward the squares. The units should measure 2" x 6½".

Make 36.

12. Join 2 units from Step 19 to 1 unit from Step18 to complete the border Star blocks. Press the seams toward the center row. Make 18. Block measures 6½" x 6½".

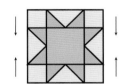

Make 18 border Star blocks.

13. Refer to the quilt assembly diagram (page 44) and alternately join 5 square-in-a-square units from Step 16 with 4 Star blocks from Step 20 to make the side borders. Make 2. Press the seams toward the square-in-a-square units. The borders should measure 6½" x 54½". Add the side borders. Press toward the green border.

14. Alternately join 5 Star blocks from Step 20 with 4 square-in-a-square units from Step 16 to make the top and bottom borders. Press as before. The borders must measure 6½" x 54½".

15. Add the top and bottom borders. Press toward the green border.

16. Layer the quilt top, batting, and backing. Baste layers together and quilt as desired.

17. Join 6 binding strips 2½" wide end-to-end and apply to the quilt (pages 36–38).

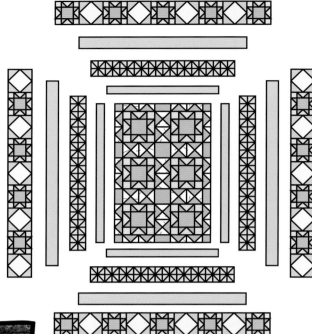

Quilt assembly

IN THE FOREST THE PANDA SLEEPS TONIGHT,
34" x 48", made by the author,
quilted by Julie Messerly,
Cedar Falls, Iowa;
AFTER APRIL'S SNOW variation
with border print borders

CYPRESS EXPRESS

CYPRESS EXPRESS, 62" x 74", made by the author, quilted by Julie Messerly, Cedar Falls, Iowa

Finished Block Size—6" x 6"

The Big Picture strategy (Strategy Four, page 15) encourages you to look at the quilt as a whole. Studying a pattern made from Cypress blocks, I realized I could get the same effect by sewing alternating columns of square-in-a-square and hourglass units.

Yardage

Background–
  2¼ yards (if using the Flip-Corner-Triangle technique)
   OR
  2½ yards (if using the Flip-Corner-Square technique)
  Green–1¾ yards
  Rust–
  ½ yard (if using the Flip-Corner-Triangle technique)
  OR
  ¾ yard (if using the Flip-Corner-Square technique)
Inner border–½ yard
Outer border–1¼ yards
Binding–⅝ yard
Backing–4¾ yards
Batting–70" x 82"

Cutting Instructions

From the background fabric:
* Cut 1 strip 9" wide. Cut 2 squares 9" x 9" (flying geese) and 3 squares 6½" x 6½" (square-in-a-square units).
* Cut 4 strips 7½" wide. Cut 20 squares 7½" x 7½" (hourglass units and flying geese)
* Cut 3 strips 6½" wide. Cut an additional 17 squares 6½" x 6½" (20 total).
* For flip-corner triangles, cut 4 strips 4" wide. Cut 32 squares 4" x 4". Cut each square once on the diagonal to make 64 **FCT**s. Cut

* This quilt is assembled in columns. Press the seam allowances open between the units in the columns and between the columns to help the quilt lie flat.

a 3½" x 3½" square from cardboard or template plastic. Cut once on the diagonal to make a marking template.
OR
* For **FCS**s, cut 6 strips 3½" wide. Cut 64 squares 3½" x 3½".

From the green fabric:
* Cut 2 strips 9" wide. Cut 5 squares 9" x 9" (flying geese wings) and 4 squares 7½" x 7½" (hourglass).
* Cut 3 strips 7½" wide. Cut an additional 13 squares 7½" x 7½" (17 total; hourglass units and flying geese).
* Cut 3 strips 6½" wide. Cut 16 squares 6½" x 6½" (square-in-a-square units).

From the rust fabric:
* Cut 4 strips 4" wide. Cut into 40 squares 4" x 4". Cut each square on the diagonal to make 80 **FCT**s.
OR
* For **FCS**s, cut 7 strips 3½" wide. Cut into 80 squares 3½" x 3½".

From the inner border fabric:
* Cut 6 strips 2½" wide.

From the outer border fabric:
• Cut 7 strips 5½" wide.

From the binding fabric:
• Cut 7 strips 2½" wide.

Sewing Instructions

1. Make 30 hourglass units (page 29) from 15 background 7½" x 7½" squares and 15 green 7½" x 7½" squares. Square-up the units to measure 6½" x 6½" (page 29).

Make 30 hourglass units.

2. Make 16 square-in-a-square units (page 27) from 16 green 6½" x 6½" squares and either 64 background **FCT**s OR 3½" x 3½" **FCS**s. The units should measure 6½" x 6½".

Make 16 green-center square-in-a-square units.

3. Make 20 square-in-a-square units from 20 background 6½" x 6½" squares and either 80 rust **FCT**s OR 3½" x 3½" **FCS**s. The units should measure 6½" x 6½".

Make 20 background-center square-in-a-square units.

4. Using the Two-Square technique (page 18), make 8 flying geese from 2 green 7½" x 7½" squares and 2 background 9" x 9" squares. The units should measure 3½" x 6½".

Make 8 green-center flying geese.

5. Using the Two-Square technique, make 20 flying geese from 5 background 7½" x 7½" squares and 5 green 9" x 9" squares. The units should measure 3½" x 6½".

Make 20 background-center flying geese.

Quilt Assembly

1. Make 2 Column A. Join 10 background-center flying geese units from Step 5.

Column A. Make 2.

2. Make 4 Column B. Alternately join 5 background-center square-in-a-square units from Step 3 with 4 green-center square-in-a-square units from Step 2. Sew a green-center flying geese unit from Step 4 to the ends of each column, paying attention to the direction of the goose body.

Column B. Make 4.

3. Make 3 Column C. Join 10 hourglass units from Step 1.

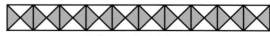

Column C. Make 3.

4. Join the columns as shown in the quilt assembly diagram (page 48) to make the quilt center. Press the seams open.

5. Join 6 inner border 2½" wide strips end-to-end. Measure, cut, and add the side borders, then the top and bottom borders (pages 34–36). Press the seams toward inner border.

6. Join 7 outer border 5½" wide strips end-to-end. Add the side outer borders, then the top and bottom borders. Press the seams toward outer border.

7. Layer quilt top, batting, and backing. Baste layers together and quilt as desired.

8. Join 7 binding 2½" wide strips end-to-end and apply to the quilt (pages 36–38).

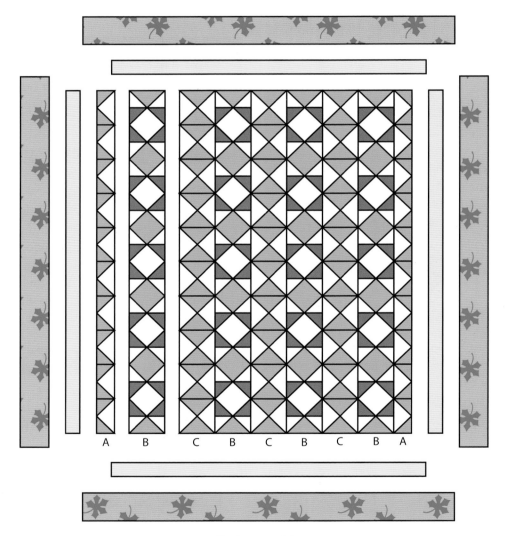

Quilt assembly

DAVE'S IDEA

DAVE'S IDEA, 52" x 66", made by the author, quilted by Julie Messerly, Cedar Falls, Iowa

Finished Block Size—8" x 8"

Do you have a great border fabric and want to show off the quilting? This is the quilt for you. I was playing with some flip-corner rectangles when my husband Dave suggested I replace some of the units with parallelograms. The result was secondary pinwheels. Blocks are made quickly using flip-corner rectangles and quadrant construction.

Yardage

Background–2½ yards
Blue flip corners–
    1 yard (if using the Flip-Corner-Triangle technique)
    OR
    1⅜ yards (if using the Flip-Corner-Square technique)
Green flip corners (for the block centers)–
    ⅝ yard (if using the Flip-Corner-Triangle technique)
    OR
    ¾ yard (if using the Flip-Corner-Square technique)
Inner border– ⅜ yard
Outer border and binding–1¾ yards
Backing–4 yards
Batting–60" x 74"

Cutting Instructions

From the background fabric:
• Cut 18 strips 4½" wide. Cut 280 rectangles 2½" x 4½".

From the blue flip-corner fabric:
• For flip-corner triangles, cut 11 strips 3" wide. Cut into 140 squares 3" x 3". Cut each square once on the diagonal to make 280 **FCT**s. Cut a 2½" x 2½" square from

Tip:

• I used the same fabric for the block center, border, and binding.

• When using the same fabric for two or more components, add together the given yardage for each component to determine the total yardage required.

• For scrap lovers, use a variety of the same color of fabric for the flip corners.

cardboard or template plastic. Cut once on the diagonal to make a marking template.
OR
• For flip-corner squares, cut 18 strips 2½". Cut into 280 **FCS**s 2½" x 2½".

From the green fabric:
• Cut 6 strips 3" wide. Cut into 70 squares 3" x 3". Cut each square on the diagonal to make 140 **FCT**s.
OR
• For **FCS**s, cut 9 strips 2½" wide. Cut into 140 squares 2½" x 2½".

From the inner border fabric:
• Cut 6 strips 2" wide.

From the outer border and binding fabric:
• Cut 7 strips 5½" wide (outer border).
• Cut 7 strips 2½" wide (binding).

Sewing Instructions

1. Make 140 right flip-corner rectangles from 140 background 2½" x 4½" rectangles and EITHER 140 blue **FCT**s OR 2½" x 2½" **FCS**s.

Make 140.

2. Make 140 right flip-corner parallelograms (page 26) from 140 background 2½" x 4½" rectangles and EITHER 140 blue and 140 green **FCT**s OR 2½" x 2½" **FCS**s in the upper-right and lower-left positions.

Make 140.

3. Sew parallelogram units from Step 2 to the left side of the flip-corner rectangles from Step 1. Press toward the flip-corner rectangle unit. The units should measure 4½" x 4½".

Make 140.

4. Join 4 units from Step 3 as shown to complete the blocks. Split-press (page 34) the center seams. The blocks should measure 8½" x 8½".

Make 35 blocks.

Quilt Assembly

1. Arrange the blocks in 7 rows of 5 blocks each as shown in the quilt assembly diagram (page 52). Press the seams in opposite directions from row to row.

2. Join the rows together to make the quilt center. Press the seams in one direction.

3. Join 6 inner border strips 2" wide end-to-end. Measure, cut, and add to the quilt (pages 34–36). Press the seams toward the inner border.

4. Join 7 outer border strips 5½" wide end-to-end. Add the outer border to the sides, then to the top and bottom. Press the seams toward the outer border.

5. Layer the quilt top, batting, and backing. Baste layers together and quilt as desired.

6. Join 7 binding 2½" wide strips end-to-end. Apply to the quilt (pages 36–38).

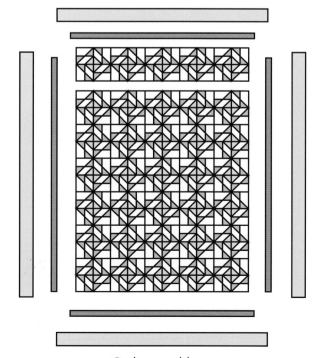

Quilt assembly

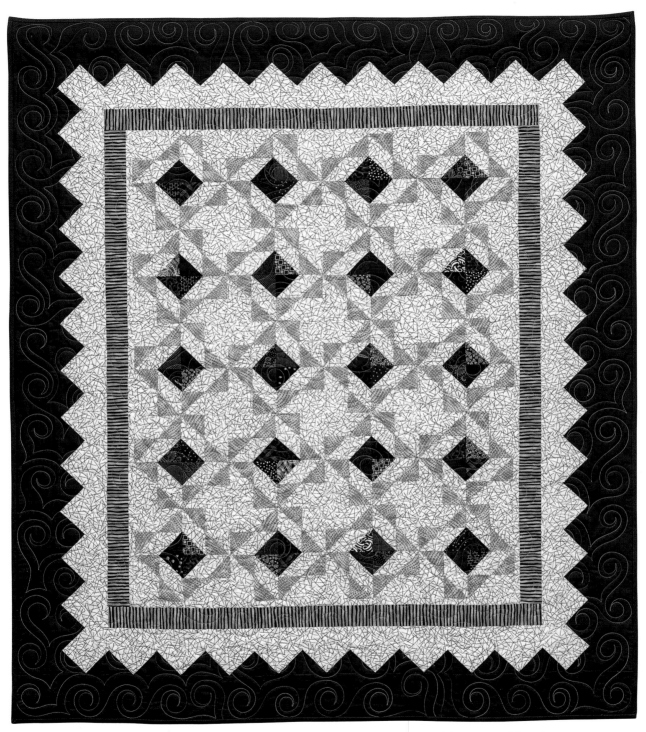

Chocolate Chip Mint Pinwheels, 52" x 60", made by the author and quilted by Lisa Hubbard & Karen Strum, Quilting Like Crazy, Cedar Falls, Iowa; Dave's Idea variation with a picket fence border

Cathy Busch ◆ Newfangled Piecing: Faster & Easier

DOUBLE CROSSING KANSAS

DOUBLE CROSSING KANSAS, 51" x 59", made by the author, quilted by Jenice Engel, Clarksville, Iowa

Finished Block Size—8" x 8"

The traditional Double X block is made from two large half-square triangles and four-patches made from two small HSTs and two small squares. I used 5" charm squares for the large HSTs and replace the four-patches with two flip-corner split rectangles. The charm pack I used was Sandhill Plums by Kansas Trouble. Double X block plus Kansas Trouble fabrics equals DOUBLE CROSSING KANSAS. I included a narrow flange between the inner and outer borders. (I'd love to have ended that sentence with "because I can!")

This quilt is in honor or all those women who went west and later decided to return to their homes in the east.

Yardage

30 Charm Squares OR ⅝ yard total of a variety of print fabrics
Background and first border–
2 yards (if using the Flip-Corner Triangle technique)
OR
2⅛ yards (if using the Flip-Corner Square technique)
Red– ⅞ yard
Outer border and binding–1½ yards
Backing–3¾ yards
Batting–59" x 67"

Cutting Instructions

From the background fabric:
- Cut 4 strips 5" wide. Cut into 30 squares 5" x 5" (HSTs).
- Cut 8 strips 2½" wide (flip-corner split rectangles).
- Cut 5 strips 2" wide (inner border).
- For the flip-corner triangles, cut 5 strips 3" wide. Cut into 60 squares 3" x 3". Cut each square once on the diagonal to make

120 **FCT**s. Cut a 2½" x 2½" square from cardboard or template plastic. Cut once on the diagonal to make a marking template.
OR
- For flip-corner squares, cut 8 strips 2½" wide. Cut 120 **FCS**s 2½" x 2½".

From the red fabric:
- Cut 8 strips 2½" wide (flip-corner split rectangles).
- Cut 6 strips 1½" wide (border flange).

From the outer border and binding fabric:
- Cut 6 strips 5" wide (outer border).
- Cut 6 strips 2½" wide (binding).

Sewing Instructions

1. Using the Two Square technique (page 18), make 60 HSTs from 30 charm squares and 30 background 5" x 5" squares. Press toward the darker fabric and trim to measure 4½" x 4½" (page 20).

Make 60 HSTs.

2. Make 8 strip-sets by sewing 1 red 2½" wide strip to 1 background 2½" strip. Press the seams toward the red fabric. The strip-sets should measure 4½" wide.

Tip:
- For your favorite sports fan, consider making the blocks in team colors and using team logo fabric for the outer border.

3. Cut the strip-sets into 120 rectangles 2½" x 4½".

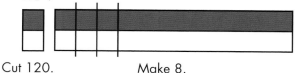

Cut 120.   Make 8.

4. Make 120 right flip-corner rectangles (page 23) using strip-set base rectangles from Step 3 and EITHER background **FCT**s OR 2½" x 2½" **FCS**s.

Make 120.

5. Make 60 four-patch units (page 7) by joining 2 units from Step 4 together. Split-press the center seams (page 34). The units should measure 4½" x 4½".

Make 60.

6. Join 2 matching half-square triangles from Step 1 and 2 four-patch units from Step 5 to complete the blocks. Press toward the HSTs and split-press the center seams. Make 30 blocks. The blocks should measure 8½" x 8½".

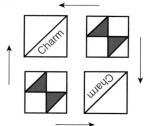

Make 30 Double X blocks.

Quilt Assembly

1. Arrange the blocks in 6 rows of 5 blocks each as shown in the quilt assembly diagram. Press the seams in opposite directions from row to row.

2. Join the rows to make quilt center. Press the seams in one direction.

3. For the inner border, join 5 background strips 2" wide end-to-end. Measure, cut, and add to the quilt (pages 34–36). Press the seams toward inner border.

4. For the flange, join 6 red strips 1½" wide end-to-end. Fold in half lengthwise and press.

5. For the outer border, join 6 border strips 5" wide end-to-end.

6. For the sides, measure and cut 2 flange strips and 2 outer borders. Pin or baste the flange into position with the folded edge toward the quilt center and the raw edges matching the inner border raw edge. Align the outer border with the raw edges. Sew through all thicknesses. Press the outer border away from the quilt top.

7. Repeat Step 6 for the top and bottom borders.

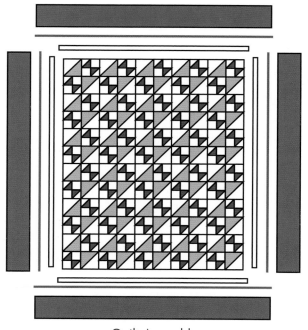

Quilt Assembly

8. Layer the quilt top, batting, and backing. Baste the layers together and quilt as desired.

9. Join 6 binding 2½" wide strips end-to-end and apply to the quilt (pages 36–38).

FAST FLIGHT TO CHINA, made by the author, quilted by Dianne Kleinschmidt, Plainfield, Iowa; DOUBLE CROSSING KANSAS variation with three fabrics used for blocks.

BUTTONS AND BOWS, made by the author, quilted by Dianne Kleinschmidt, Plainfield, Iowa; DOUBLE CROSSING KANSAS variation with flip-corner split rectangles made with a charm square pack.

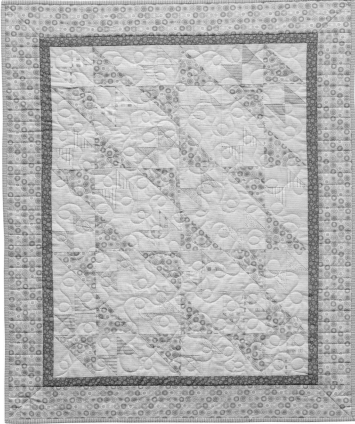

Cathy Busch ◈ Newfangled Piecing: Faster & Easier

Every Quilter Needs a Lynn

Every Quilter Needs a Lynn, 80" x 80", made by the author, quilted by Julie Messerly, Cedar Falls, Iowa

Finished Block Size—12" x 12"

The pink, brown, and cream fabric in quilt reminded me of Neapolitan ice cream. The title was going to be some play on Naples or ice cream; that is, until I got to the inner border. The fabric I brought to the retreat didn't work. Co-retreater, Lynn, showed me a pink strip she had used in one of her Farmer's Wife blocks. It was perfect. She said she had more at home. Lynn called her daughter, met her on the road, and ta-da—my inner border. I realized that every quilter needs a Lynn or to be a Lynn. One of my favorite things about quilting is the support fellow quilters provide, and not just in the form of inner border fabric.

Yardage

Background–4½ yards
Pink print–¾ yard
    ⅝ yard (if using the Flip-Corner Triangle technique)
    OR
    ¾ yard (if using the Flip-Corner Square technique)
Brown–
    1 yard (if using the Flip-Corner Triangle technique)
    OR
    1¼ yards (if using the Flip-Corner-Square technique)
Bright pink accent–½ yard
Green–¼ yard
Inner border–⅜ yard
Outer border and binding–2½ yards (cut from the length of the fabric)
Backing–7¼ yards
Batting–88" x 88"

- I use diagonal seam when joining strips of fabric EXCEPT when working with striped fabric. To eliminate the frustration of trying to match the stripes, I use a straight seam.

Cutting Instructions

From the background fabric:

- Cut 1 strip 18½" wide. Cut 2 squares 18½" x 18½". Cut each square twice on the diagonal to make 8 side setting triangles.

- Cut 1 strip 19" wide. Referring to cutting diagram, cut 1 square 18½" x 18½". Cut each square twice on the diagonal to make 4 side setting triangles (12 total). Cut 2 squares 9½" x 9½". Cut each square once on the diagonal to make 4 corner setting triangles. From remainder of the strip, cut 6 squares 6" x 6" (flying geese wings).

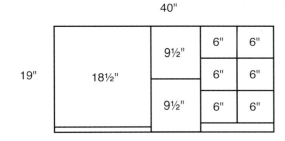

Cutting diagram

- Cut 2 strips 8" wide. Cut into 8 squares 8" x 8" (half-square triangles).
- Cut 6 strips 6½" wide. Cut into 64 rectangles 3½" x 6½" (flip-corner rectangles).

- Cut 1 strip 6" wide. Cut an additional 3 squares 6" x 6" (12 total; flying geese wings).
- Cut 5 strips 3½" wide. Cut into 16 squares 3½" x 3½" (square-in-a-square centers) and 36 rectangles 2" x 3½" (top and bottom of the square-in-a-square units and the top of the four-patch units).
- Cut 4 strips 3½" wide (strip-sets).
- Cut 4 strips 2" wide (four-patch unit strip-sets).

From the pink print:
- Cut 2 strips 8" wide. Cut into 8 squares 8" x 8".
- For flip-corner triangles, cut 2 strips 2½" wide. Cut into 32 squares 2½" x 2½". Cut each square once on the diagonal to make 64 **FCT**s. Cut a 2" square from cardboard or template plastic. Cut once on the diagonal to make a marking template.

OR
- For flip-corner squares, cut 4 strips 2" wide. Cut into 64 **FCS**s 2" x 2".

From the brown fabric:
- Cut 1 strip 4½" wide. Cut into 9 squares 4½" x 4½" (flying geese centers).
- Cut 1 strip 2" wide (four-patch strip-set).
- Cut 11 strips 2½" wide. Cut into 164 squares 2½" x 2½". Cut each square once on the diagonal to make 328 **FCT**s.

OR
- For **FCS**s cut 17 strips 2" wide into 328 squares 2" x 2".

From the bright pink accent fabric:
- Cut 7 strips 2" wide.

From the green fabric:
- Cut 4 strips 2" wide.

From the inner border fabric:
- Cut 7 strips 1½" wide.

Outer border and binding strips are cut from the length of fabric after quilt center is completed.

Sewing Instructions

Block A

1. Make 64 half-square triangles, using the Super-Sized technique (page 18), from 8 background 8" x 8" squares and 8 pink print 8" x 8" squares. Trim to measure 3½" x 3½" (pages 18–19).

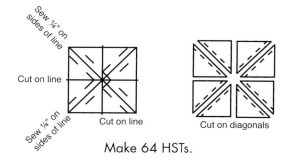

Make 64 HSTs.

2. Make 64 four flip-corner rectangles (page 21–22) from 64 background rectangles 3½" x 6½" and EITHER 256 brown **FCT**s OR 2" x 2" **FCS**s.

Make 64.

3. Make 16 square-in-a-square (page 27) units from 16 background 3½" x 3½" squares and EITHER 64 pink print **FCT**s OR 2" x 2" **FCS**s.

Make 16.

4. Sew 2" x 3½" background rectangles to the top and bottom of each square-in-a-square unit from Step 3. Press toward the background rectangle. The units should measure 3½" x 6½".

Make 16.

5. Make 2 strip-sets by sewing 3½" background strip between 2 green 2" strips. Press the seams toward the background strip. The strip-set should measure 6½" wide. Cut the strip-sets into 32 rectangles 2" x 6½".

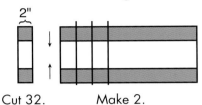

Cut 32.   Make 2.

6. Sew strip-set rectangles from Step 5 to the sides of each unit from Step 4. Press the seams toward the strip-set rectangles. The units should measure 6½" x 6½".

Make 16.

7. For the top and bottom rows of the blocks, sew half-square triangles from Step 1 to both sides of 32 four-flip-corner rectangles from Step 2. Press the seams away from the center. The units should measure 12½" x 3½".

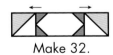

Make 32.

8. For the center row, sew the remaining 32 four-flip-corner rectangles from Step 2 to both sides of the center unit from Step 6. Press the seams toward the center. The units should measure 12½" x 6½".

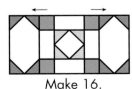

Make 16.

9. Join the top and bottom rows from Step 7 to the center units from Step 8 to complete Block A. Press the seams toward top and bottom rows. The blocks should measure 12½" x 12½".

Make 16 Block A.

Block B

10. Make 36 flying geese, using the Two Square technique (page 18), from 9 background 6" x 6" squares and 9 brown 4½" x 4½" squares. The units should measure 2" x 3½".

Make 36.

11. Make 36 adjacent flip-corner squares from 36 background 3½" x 3½" squares and EITHER 72 brown **FCT**s OR 2" x 2" **FCS**s.

Make 36.

12. Sew flying geese from Step 10 to the top of the flip-corner squares from Step 11. Press toward the flying geese units. The units should measure 3½" x 5".

Make 36.

13. Make 4 strip-sets by sewing background 2" strips to bright pink 2" strips. Press toward the bright pink strip. The strip-sets should

measure 3½" wide. Cut the strip-sets into 72 rectangles 2" x 3½".

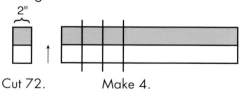

Cut 72.   Make 4.

14. Pair units from Step 13 to make 36 four-patch units. Split-press (page 34) the seams. The units should measure 3½" x 3½".

Make 36.

15. Sew 2" x 3½" background rectangles to top of each unit from Step 14. Press the seams toward the background rectangle. The units should measure 3½" x 5".

Make 36.

16. Make 2 strip-sets by sewing together back-ground 3½" strip and bright pink 2" strip. Press the seams toward the background strip. The strip-sets should measure 5" wide. Cut into 36 rectangles 2" x 5".

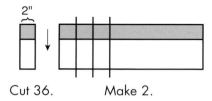

Cut 36.   Make 2.

17. Sew units from Step 16 to the right side of units from Step 15. Press the seams toward strip-set. The units should measure 5" x 5".

Make 36.

18. Make 1 strip-set from 2" brown and 2" bright pink strips. Press the seams toward the brown strip. The strip-set should measure 3½" wide. Cut into 18 rectangles 2" x 3½".

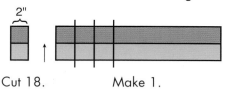

Cut 18.   Make 1.

19. Pair units from Step 18 to make 9 four-patch units. Split-press the seams. The units should measure 3½" x 3½".

Make 9.

20. For the top and bottom rows, sew 1 unit from Step 17 to each side of 18 units from Step 12. Press the seams away from the center. The units should measure 3½" x 12½".

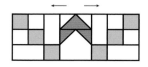

Make 18.

21. For the center rows, sew 1 unit from Step 12 to each side of the four-patch units from Step 19. Press the seams toward the center. The units should measure 5" x 12½".

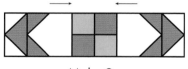

Make 9.

22. Join the top and bottom rows from Step 11 to the center rows from Step 12 to complete Block B. Press the seams toward the top and bottom rows. The blocks should measure 12½" x 12½".

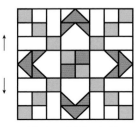

Make 9 Block B.

Quilt Assembly

1. Arrange the blocks, side setting triangles, and corner setting triangles in diagonal rows as indicated in the quilt assembly diagram.

2. Join the diagonal rows. Press the seams toward Block A.

3. Join the rows together. Press the seams in one direction.

4. Straighten quilt edges (page 36).

5. Join 7 inner border 2" wide strips end-to-end. Measure, cut, and add the inner border (pages 34–36).

6. Measure the length of the quilt, cut 2 outer side borders 6½" wide from the LENGTH of the border fabric, and add to the sides. Press the seams toward the outer border.

7. Measure the width of the quilt, cut 2 outer top and bottom borders 6½" wide from the LENGTH of border fabric, and add to the quilt. Press seams toward outer border.

8. Layer the quilt top, batting, and backing. Baste the layers together and quilt as desired.

9. Cut 2½" wide binding strips from the LENGTH of the border fabric and apply to the quilt (pages 36–38).

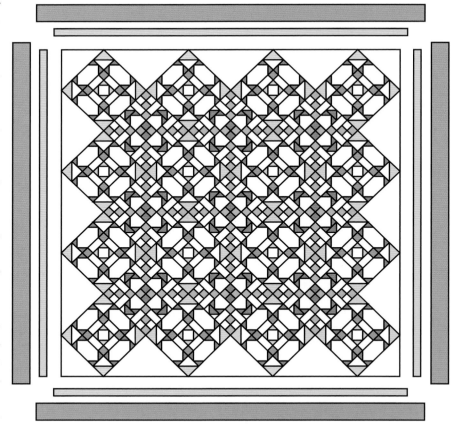

Quilt assembly

TEQUILA, LIMES, AND FROG LEGS, 62" x 80", made by the author, quilted by Jenice Engel, Clarksville, Iowa; smaller version of EVERY QUILTER NEEDS A LYNN

GEESE IN THE VINEYARD

GEESE IN THE VINEYARD, 80" x 92", made by the author, quilted by Julie Messerly, Cedar Falls, Iowa

Cathy Busch ◆ Newfangled Piecing: Faster & Easier

Finished Block Size—9" x 9"

Dave and I had been touring Iowa wineries. When I found a batik fabric with grape motifs and a fat quarter bundle with purples and greens, I decided to make a quilt as a remembrance of our trip. The Eccentric Star blocks are made using the partial seam technique from four flying geese and a center square. The flying geese in the inner borders soar around the center stars.

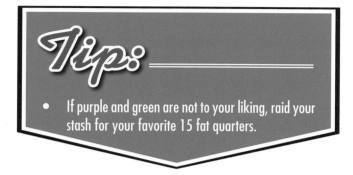

Tip:

- If purple and green are not to your liking, raid your stash for your favorite 15 fat quarters.

Yardage

Background–3 yards
15 fat quarters (flying geese)
Sashing and inner border–1¼ yards
Cornerstones and third border–½ yard
Outer border and binding–2½ yards
Backing–5½ yards
Batting–88" x 100"

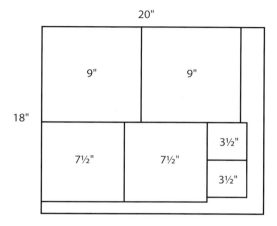

Cutting diagram A

Cutting Instructions

From the background fabric:
- Cut 6 strips 9" wide. Cut 22 squares 9" x 9" (border flying geese wings).
- Cut 6 strips 7½" wide. Cut 30 squares 7½" x 7½" (block flying geese centers).

From 7 fat quarters:
- Referring to cutting diagram A, cut 2 squares 9" x 9" (block flying geese wings), 2 squares 7½" x 7½" (border flying geese body) and 2 squares 3½" x 3½" (block center).

From 8 fat quarters:
- Referring to cutting diagram B, cut 2 squares 9" x 9" (block flying geese wings), square 7½" x 7½" (border flying geese body) and 2 squares 3½" x 3½" (block center).

Total 30 squares 9" x 9", 30 squares 3½" x 3½", and 33 squares 7½" x 7½".

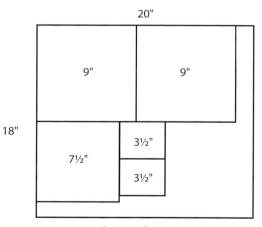

Cutting diagram B

From the sashing and inner border fabric:
- Cut 2 strips 9½" wide. From 1 strip cut 20 rectangles 2" x 9½". (The remaining strip is used for the cornerstone/sashing strip-set.)

- Cut 3 strips 2" wide. Cut 9 rectangles 2" x 9½".
- Cut 3 strips 2¾" wide (inner top and bottom borders).
- Cut 3 strips 2" wide (inner side borders).

From the cornerstones and third border fabric:
- Cut 1 strip 2" wide (cornerstones).
- Cut 8 strips 1½" wide (third border).

The outer border and binding strips are cut from the length of fabric after the quilt center is completed.

Sewing Instructions

1. Using the Two-Square technique (page 18), make 120 flying geese from 30 fat quarter 9" x 9" squares and 30 background 7½" x 7½" squares.

Make 120.

2. Using partial seam construction (page 13), make 30 blocks from 3½" x 3½" center squares and matching flying geese units. Press the seams away from the center square. The blocks should measure 9½" x 9½".

Make 30.

3. Sew 2" x 9½" sashing strips to the right side of 24 blocks. Press the seams toward the sashing strips. The units should measure 9½" x 11". (You will have 6 blocks and 5 sashing strips remaining.)

Make 24.

4. Make a strip-set from a 2" cornerstone strips and a 9½" sashing strip. Press the seams toward the sashing strip. Cut 20 rectangles 2" x 11".

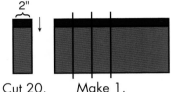

Cut 20.   Make 1.

5. Sew 1 unit from Step 4 to the bottom of each unit from Step 3. Press the seams toward the sashing. The units should measure 11" x 11".

Make 24.

6. Sew 1 sashing 2" x 9½" strip to the bottom of 5 blocks from Step 2. Press seams toward sashing strips. The units should measure 9½" x 11". (You will have 1 block remaining.)

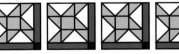

Make 5.

7. Join 4 units from Step 5 to 1 unit from Step 6 to make a row. Press the seams toward the sashing strips. Make 5 rows. The rows should measure 11" x 51½".

  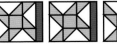

Make 5 rows.

8. For the bottom row, join 4 units from Step 3 to the remaining unsashed block. Press the seams toward sashing strips. The row should measure 9½" x 51½".

Make 1 bottom row.

9. Join the rows to make the quilt center as shown in the quilt assembly diagram (page 68). Press the seams in one direction. For the pieced borders to fit, the quilt center must measure 51½" x 62".

10. Join 3 inner side border 2" wide strips together end to end. Cut 2 side borders 62" long and add to the quilt center (pages 34–36). Press the seams toward the inner border.

11. Join 3 inner border 2¾" wide strips end to end. Cut the top and bottom borders 54½" long and add to the quilt center. Press the seams toward the inner border. The quilt center should measure 54½" x 66½".

12. Using the Two Square technique, make 88 flying geese from 22 background 9" x 9" squares and 22 fat quarter 7½" x 7½" squares.

Make 88.

13. Make 4 pieced borders by joining 22 flying geese (see the quilt assembly diagram, page 68). Press the seams away from the point. The borders should measure 6½" x 66½".

Make 4.

14. Add the side pieced border strips paying attention to the direction of the geese. Press toward the inner border.

15. Add the top and bottom pieced border strips, paying attention to the direction of the geese. Press toward the inner border.

16. Join 8 third border 1½" wide strips end-to-end. Measure, cut, and add to the quilt. Press the seams toward the third border.

17. Measure the length of the quilt. Cut two outer side borders 6½" wide from the LENGTH of fabric and attach to the quilt. Press the seams toward the outer border.

18. Measure the width of the quilt. Cut the outer top and bottom borders 6½" wide from the LENGTH of fabric and attach to the quilt. Press the seams toward the outer border.

19. Layer quilt top, batting, and backing. Baste layers together and quilt as desired.

20. Cut 2½" binding strips from the LENGTH of fabric and join end-to-end. Apply to the quilt (page 36–38).

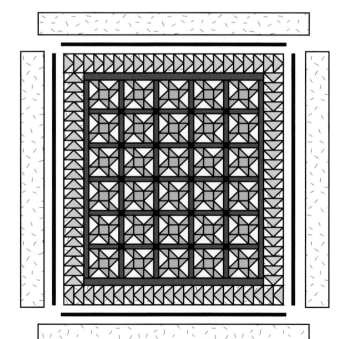

Quilt assembly

FLYING PADDLES, 33" x 42", made by Debbie Fetch, quilted by Julie Messerly, Cedar Falls, Iowa;
GEESE IN THE VINEYARD variation made without sashing

ISLAND AUTUMN

ISLAND AUTUMN, 70" x 82", made by the author, quilted by Julie Messerly, Cedar Falls, Iowa

Finished Block Size—7½" x 7½"

My friend Barb made a quilt of foundation-pieced Leaf blocks set with Log Cabin blocks. I decided I needed a quilt to festoon my bed between harvest time and the holidays. I selected batiks for the leaves. To simplify the piecing, I eliminated seams from the Leaf block. To simplify cutting, I used a right-angle ruler to make the half-square triangles.

Yardage

Note: The cutting directions are designed for the Right-Angle-Ruler technique to make half-square triangles. If you choose a different method, you may need more yardage.

Background—1¾ yards
Leaves—11 fat eights (9" x 20")
Stem—1 fat quarter
Sashing and inner border—1½ yards
Cornerstones—⅛ yard
Outer border and binding—2¼ yards
Backing—5
Batting—78" x 90"

Cutting Instructions

From the background fabric:
- Cut 2 strips 14" wide.
- From each strip cut squares referring to cutting diagram A.
- Cut 2 squares 14" x 14". Cut each square twice on the diagonal to make side setting triangles (16 total; you will have 2 extra triangles).
- Cut 1 square 7¼" x 7¼". Cut each square once on the diagonal to make corner setting triangles.
- Cut 3 squares 3" x 3" (block corner squares; 6 total).

Tip:

- Setting blocks on point gets you more quilt for the number of blocks made.

- Thirty-two 7½" blocks set on point, as shown in this quilt, with 1½" sashing results in a 53" x 65¾" quilt center.

- Thirty 7½" blocks set straight in 6 rows of 5 blocks each with 1½" sashing results in a 46½" x 55½" quilt center.

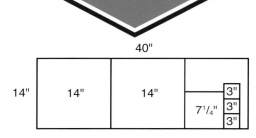

Cutting diagram A

- Cut 2 strips 3" wide. Cut an additional 26 squares 3" x 3" (block corner squares; 32 total).
- Cut 3 strips 3"wide (half-square triangles).
- Cut 3 strips 3½" wide. Cut into 32 squares 3½" x 3½" (stem corner squares).
- For flip-corner triangles, cut 3 strips 3½" wide. Cut into 32 squares 3½" x 3½" squares. Cut each square once on the diagonal to make 64 **FCT**s. Cut a 3" x 3" square from cardboard or template plastic. Cut on the diagonal to make marking template.

OR
- For flip-corner squares, cut 5 strips 3" wide. Cut into 64 **FCS**s 3" x 3".

From the leaf fabric:

- Cut 3 leaves per EACH fat eighth. (You will have one extra leaf.) Cut 3 strips 3" wide. Cut into 3 rectangles 3" x 8" and 3 rectangles 3" x 5½" as shown in cutting diagram B. The remainder will be used to make half-square triangles.

20"

3 x 8"	5½"	5½"	
3 x 8"	8"		
3 x 5½"	Strip for		

9"

Cutting diagram B

From the stem fabric:

Cut 2 strips 5" wide. Cut into 32 rectangles ¾" x 5".

From the sashing and inner border fabric:

- Cut 4 strips 8" wide. Cut into 46 rectangles 2" x 8". (The remaining strip and partial strip are used for the sashing/cornerstone strip-sets.)
- Cut 1 strip 2" wide. Cut into 2 rectangles 2" x 11".
- Cut 6 strips 2" wide (inner border).

From the cornerstone fabric:

Cut two 2 strips 2" wide.

Sewing Instructions

Stem Units

1. For the stem units, cut 3½" x 3½" background squares once on the diagonal.

2. With right sides together, sew a ¾" x 5" stem rectangle to one side of each triangle. Press the seam toward stem.

3. With right sides together, sew a second triangle to the other side of the stems. Press the seam toward the stem.

4. Square-up the stem units to 3" x 3" (page 20).

Make 32 stem units.

5. Use the Right-Angle-Ruler technique (page 17), the remaining 3" leaf strips from each fat eighth, and the 3" background strips to make 64 HSTs—6 HSTs for each of 10 leaf colors and 4 HSTs of the last leaf color.

Make 64.

6. Join 2 half-square triangles to make a half-square triangle pair.

Make 32.

7. Join a 3" x 3" background square to the half-square triangle pairs from Step 7. Press the seams toward the background square. The units should measure 3" x 8".

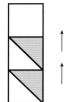

Make 32.

8. For the center column, make 32 right flip-corner rectangles (page 23) from 3" x 8" leaf fabric rectangles and EITHER background **FCT**s OR 3" x 3" **FCS**s.

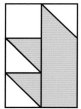

Make 32.

9. Join the units from Step 8 to the left side of the units from Step 9. The units should measure 5½" x 8".

Make 32.

10. Make 32 right flip-corner rectangles from 3" x 5½" leaf fabric rectangles and EITHER 32 background **FCT**s OR 3" x 3" **FCS**s.

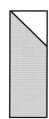

Make 32.

11. For the right column, sew stem units from Step 5 to the bottom of the rectangle units from Step 11. Press the seams away from the stem unit. The units should measure 3" x 8".

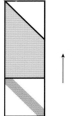

Make 32.

12. Join units from Step 12 to the right side of the units from Step 10 to complete the Leaf blocks. Press the seams toward the center column. The blocks should measure 8" x 8".

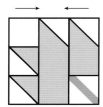

Make 32 Leaf blocks.

Quilt Assembly

The quilt is constructed in diagonal rows. Follow the step-by-step row construction and refer to the quilt assembly diagram (page 74). Pay close attention to the orientation of the setting triangles as you make each row.

In constructing the rows, always press toward the sashing strips and the setting triangles.

1. Make 2 strip-sets with 2" cornerstone fabric strips and 8" sashing fabric strips. Press the seams toward the sashing fabric. Cut into 31 cornerstone/sashing rectangles 2" x 9½".

Cut 31.   Make 2.

Row 1

- Sew 2 sashing 2" x 8" rectangles to opposite sides of 1 Leaf block.
- Sew a 2" x 11" sashing strip to the top.
- Sew 2 side setting triangles to the ends of the row.
- Sew a corner setting triangle to the top.

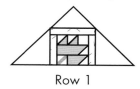

Row 1

Row 2

- Sew 1 sashing 2" x 8" rectangle between 2 cornerstone/sashing rectangles from Step 1.
- Alternately sew 4 sashing 2" x 8" rectangles and 3 Leaf blocks.
- Sew the sashing strip to the TOP of the block strip.
- Sew 1 side setting triangle to each end of the row.

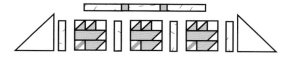

Row 3

- Join 4 cornerstone/sashing rectangles from Step 1 and 1 sashing 2" x 8" rectangle.
- Alternately sew 6 sashing 2" x 8" rectangles and 5 Leaf blocks.
- Sew the sashing strip to the TOP of the block strip.
- Sew 1 side setting triangle to each end of the row.

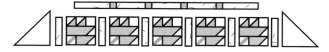

Row 4

- Join 6 cornerstone/sashing rectangles from Step 1 and 1 sashing 2" x 8" rectangle.
- Alternately sew 8 sashing 2" x 8" rectangles and 7 Leaf blocks.

- Sew the sashing strip to the TOP of the block strip.
- Sew 1 side setting triangle to left end of the row and 1 corner setting triangle to the right end.

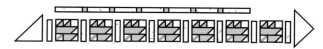

Row 5

- Join 7 cornerstone/sashing rectangles from Step 1 and 1 sashing 2" x 8" rectangle.

Row 6

- Join 6 cornerstone/sashing strips from Step 1 and 1 sashing 2" x 8" strip.
- Alternately sew 7 sashing 2" x 8" rectangles and 7 Leaf blocks.
- Sew the sashing strip to the BOTTOM of the block strip.
- Sew 1 side setting triangle to right end of the row and a corner setting triangle to the left end.

Row 7

- Join 4 cornerstone/sashing strips Step 1 and 1 sashing 2" x 8" rectangle.
- Alternately sew 6 sashing 2" x 8" rectangles and 5 Leaf blocks.
- Sew the sashing strip to the BOTTOM of the block strip.
- Sew 1 side setting triangle to each end of the row.

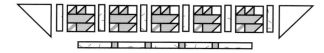

Row 8

- Sew 1 sashing 2" x 8" strip between 2 cornerstone/sashing strips from Step 1.

- Alternately sew 4 sashing 2" x 8" rectangles and 3 Leaf blocks.
- Sew the sashing strip to BOTTOM of the block strip.
- Sew 1 side setting triangle to each end of the row.

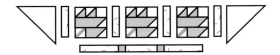

Row 9

- Sew 1 sashing 2" x 8" strip to each side of 1 leaf block.
- Sew a 2" x 11" sashing strip to the bottom of the block row.
- Sew 2 side setting triangles to the ends of the row.
- Sew a corner setting triangle to the BOTTOM of the row.

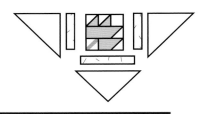

Quilt Assembly

1. Join the rows to complete the quilt top. Straighten the edges (page 34).

2. Join 6 inner border 2" wide strips end-to-end with 45-degree seams. Measure, cut, and add to the quilt (pages 34–36). Press toward the inner border.

3. Measure for the side borders (pages 34–36) and cut from the length of fabric. Add to the quilt top. Measure for the top and bottom borders and cut from the length of fabric. Add to the quilt top.

4. Layer quilt top, batting, and binding. Baste layers together and quilt as desired.

5. Cut 2½" binding strips from the length of fabric (you need a minimum of 320") Join end-to-end and apply to the quilt (pages 36–38).

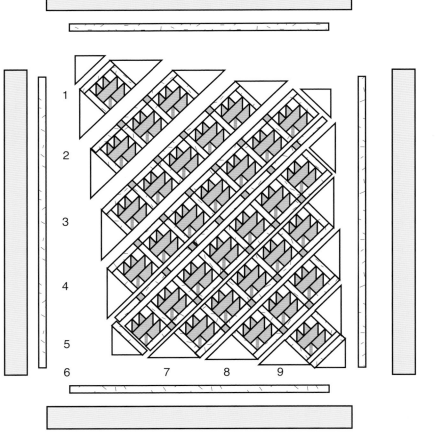

Quilt assembly

MEMORIES OF EILEEN

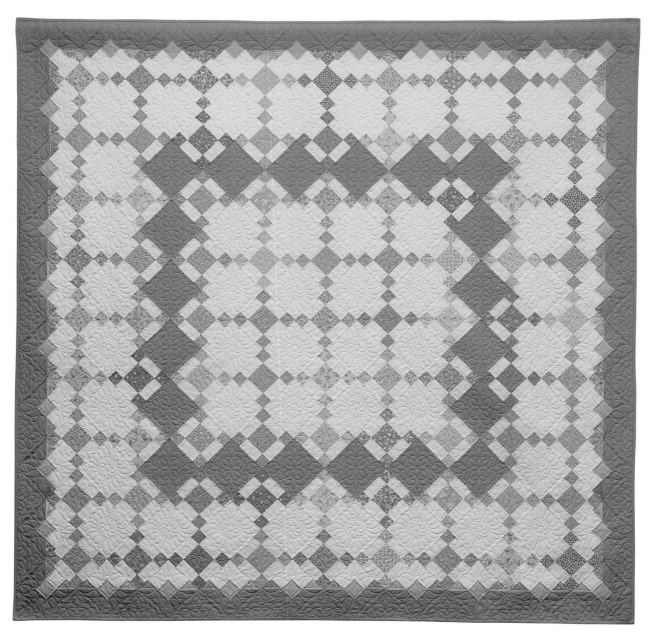

MEMORIES OF EILEEN, 85" x 85", made by the author, quilted by Julie Messerly, Cedar Falls, Iowa

Finished Block Size—6" x 6"
81 Uneven Nine-Patch blocks
64 setting blocks
32 border blocks, and 4 corner blocks

I was cleaning in my studio when I got the news of my quilting friend Eileen's passing. Wanting to make a remembrance quilt I selected 30s prints. The whimsical prints combined with my memories of Eileen warmed my heart.

Yardage

White—3¾ yards (for background, border blocks, and setting squares)

Green—3½ (setting squares, border, and binding)

Medium prints—2¼+ yards of scraps (blocks)

Peach—¼ yard (border blocks)

Backing—2¾ yard 120" wide backing or 7¾ yards

Batting—93" x 93"

Cutting Instructions

From the white background fabric:
- Cut 15 strips 4" wide. Cut into 162 rectangles 3½" x 4".
- Cut 8 strips 6½" wide. Cut into 44 squares 6½" x 6½" (setting squares).
- Cut 3 strips 2½" wide (border block strip-sets).
- Cut 2 strips 4½" wide. Cut into 32 rectangles 2½" x 4½" (border blocks).

From the medium print scraps:
- For blocks, cut 1 square 3½" x 3½" and 1 square 4" x 4" from the same fabric to make a pair. Make a total of 81 pairs.

- For border flip-corner triangles, cut 40 squares 3" x 3". Cut each square once on

the diagonal to make 40 **FCT**s. Cut a 2½" x 2½" square from cardboard of template plastic. Cut once on the diagonal to make a marking template.

OR
- For border flip-corner squares, cut 80 **FCS**s 2½" x 2½".

From the green fabric:
- Cut 3 strips 6½" wide. Cut into 40 rectangles 2½" x 6½" (border blocks).
- Cut 3 strips 4½" wide. Cut into 40 rectangles 2½" x 4½" (border blocks).
- Cut 4 strips 6½" wide. Cut 20 squares 6½" x 6½" (setting squares).
- Cut 1 strip 2½" wide. Cut 4 squares 2½" x 2½" (corner border blocks).
- Cut 3 strips 9¾" wide. Cut 9 squares 9¾" x 9¾". Cut each square on both diagonals to make 36 side setting triangles.
- Cut 1 strip 5¼" wide. Cut 2 squares 5¼" x 5¼". Cut each square on one diagonal to make 4 corner setting triangles.
- Cut 9 strips 2½" wide for binding.

From the peach border square fabric:
- Cut 3 strips 2½" wide (border block strip-sets).

Sewing Instructions

Uneven Nine-Patch Blocks

1. Sew each medium print 3½" x 3½" square to a background 3½" x 4" rectangle. Press toward square. The units should measure 3½" x 7".

Make 81.

2. Sew each medium print 4" x 4" square to a background 3½" x 4" rectangle. Press toward the square. The units should measure 4" x 7".

Make 81.

3. Join units from Step 1 to the units from Step 2. Split-press the seams open (page 34). The units should measure 7" x 7".

Make 81.

4. Cut a 1¾" segment from the Step 3 units as shown.

Make 81.

5. Sew the cut segment to opposite side of the unit. Split-press the seams open. The units should measure 6½" x 7".

Make 81.

6. Cut a 1¾" segment from the Step 5 units as shown.

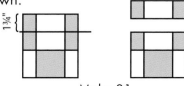

Make 81.

7. Sew the cut segment to the opposite side to complete the blocks. The blocks should measure 6½" x 6½".

Make 81.

Border Blocks

8. Make 32 right flip-corner rectangles from green 2½" x 6½" rectangles and EITHER print **FCT**s OR 2½" x 2½" **FCS**s.

Make 32.

9. Make 32 left flip-corner rectangles from green 2½" x 4½" rectangles and EITHER **FCT**s OR 2½" x 2½" **FCS**s.

Make 32.

10. Make 3 strip-sets from 2½" background and 2½" peach strips. Press the seams toward

the peach fabric. Cut into 36 rectangles 2½" x 4½". (Note: 4 strip-set rectangles will be used for corner blocks.)

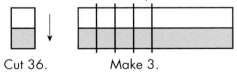

Cut 36.   Make 3.

11. Sew 32 background 2½" x 4½" rectangles to the left side of the strip-set rectangles from Step 3. Press toward the strip-set rectangles. The units should measure 4½" x 4½".

Make 32.

12. Sew flip-corner rectangles from Step 2 to the right side of the units from Step 4. Press toward the strip set rectangles. The units should measure 4½" x 6½".

Make 32.

13. Sew flip-corner rectangles from Step 1 to bottom of units from Step 5 to finish the blocks. Press toward the center. The blocks should measure 6½" x 6½".

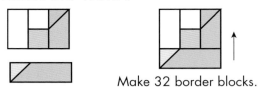

Make 32 border blocks.

Corner Blocks

14. Make 4 right flip-corner rectangles from green border 2½" x 6½" rectangles and EITHER print **FCT**s OR 2½" x 2½" **FCS**s.

Make 4.

15. Make 4 left flip-corner rectangles from green border 2½" x 6½" rectangles and EITHER print **FCT**s OR 2½" x 2½" **FCS**s.

Make 4.

16. Sew 2½" x 2½" green squares to the 4 remaining strip-set rectangles. Press toward the peach square.

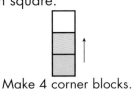

Make 4 corner blocks.

17. Sew right flip-corner rectangles from Step 1 to strip-set units from Step 3. Press toward the strip-set rectangles. The units should measure 4½" x 6½".

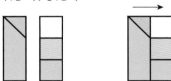

18. Sew left flip-corner rectangles from Step 3 to the units from Step 4 to complete the blocks. Press toward the strip-set rectangles. The blocks should measure 6½" x 6½".

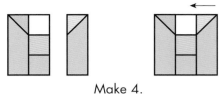

Make 4.

Quilt Assembly

1. Arrange the blocks, corner blocks, setting squares, and setting triangles in diagonal rows as shown in the quilt assembly diagram. Join the blocks into rows. Press the seams toward the setting squares and triangles. Join the diagonal rows together. Press the seams toward the solid squares.

2. Straighten the quilt edges (page 34).

3. Layer the quilt top, batting, and backing. Baste layers together and quilt as desired.

4. Join 9 binding 2½" strips end-to-end and apply to the quilt (pages 36–38).

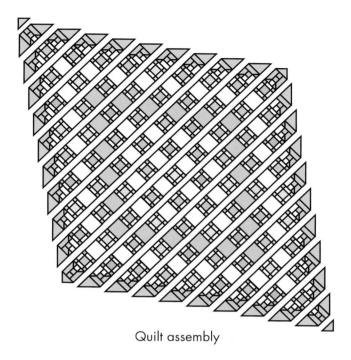

Quilt assembly

MOROCCAN TILES, 53" x 61", made by the author, quilted by Dianne Kleinschmidt, Plainfield, Iowa; MEMORIES OF EILEEN variation with a straight print border

QUICK KITTENS, 42½" x 51", made by the author, quilted by Julie Messerly, Cedar Falls, Iowa; MEMORIES OF EILEEN variation; baby quilt in bright colors with a pieced border

NORTH AND SOUTH

NORTH AND SOUTH, 50" x 66", made by Diane Yarcho, quilted by Julie Messerly, Cedar Falls, Iowa

Cathy Busch ◆ Newfangled Piecing: Faster & Easier

Finished Block Size—8" x 8"

I won a stack of Civil War fat quarters. Not really my style of fabric. Luckily, my friend Diane enjoys working with reproduction fabrics. I developed a pattern made up of positive and negative blocks and she made the quilt. She used flip-corner squares to make the square-in-a-square units and made "waste-not want-not" half-square triangles. From these half-square triangles she made two tiny quilts. Following the directions, you end up with one extra light block. Can you say instant label?

Yardage

Background–2⅝ yards (if using the Flip-Corner Triangle technique)
    OR
    2¾ yards (if using the Flip-Corner Square technique)
Medium-to-dark prints–18 fat quarters
Binding–½ yard
Backing–3¼ yards
Batting –58" x 74"

Cutting Instructions

From the background fabric:
- Cut 4 strips 7" wide. Cut into 18 squares 7" x 7" (flying geese wings in the positive blocks).
- Cut 3 strips 5½" wide. Cut into 17 squares 5½" x 5½" squares (flying geese centers in the negative blocks).
- Cut 3 strips 4½" wide. Cut into 18 squares 4½" x 4½" (square-in-a-square centers in the positive blocks).
- For flip-corner triangles (square-in-a-square units in the negative blocks), cut 3 strips 3" wide. Cut into 34 squares 3" x 3". Cut each square once on the diagonal to make 68 **FCT**s. Cut a 2½" x 2½" square from cardboard or template plastic. Cut once on the diagonal to

> **Tips:**
> - Piano Key borders sometimes are not the same length as the quilt. Increase or decrease the seam allowances between a few of the rectangles until the borders and the quilt sides are equal.
> - Baste a scant ¼" from the edge of the quilt to keep the pieced border seams from separating during quilting.

make a marking template.
OR
- For flip-corner squares, cut 5 strips 2½" wide. Cut into 68 **FCS**s 2½" x 2½".
- Cut 5 strips 2½" wide. Cut 68 square 2½" x 2½" (corners of the negative blocks).
- Cut 5 strips 1½" wide (inner border).

From EACH fat quarter print:
- Cut 1 strip 7" wide. Cut into 1 square 7" x 7" (flying geese wings in the negative blocks; 18 total; you'll have 1 extra), 1 square 5½" x 5½" (flying geese centers in the positive blocks; 18 total), and 1 square 4½" x 4½" (square-in-a-square centers in the negative blocks; 18 total; you'll have one extra).
- Cut 1 strip 3" wide. Cut into 2 squares 3" x 3". Cut each square once on the diagonal to make 4 **FCT**s (for square-in-a-square units in the positive blocks; 72 total)
OR
- For **FCS**s, cut 1 strip 2½" wide. Cut into 8 squares 2½" x 2½" (flip-corner squares and corner squares for the positive blocks).
- Cut 1 strip 2½" wide. Cut 4 squares 2½" x 2½" (corner squares for the positive blocks; 72 total).

- Cut 1 strip 4½" wide. Cut 6 rectangles 2½" x 4½" (pieced outer border; 108 total).

From the binding fabric:
- Cut 6 strips 2½" wide.

Sewing Instructions

Positive Blocks

1. Make 72 flying geese, using the Two-Square technique (page 18) from background 7" x 7" squares and print 5½" x 5½" squares. The units should measure 2½" x 4½".

Make 72.

2. Make 18 square-in-a-square units (page 27) from background 4½" x 4½" squares and EITHER 4 print **FCT**s OR 2½" x 2½" **FCS**s.

Make 18.

3. For the top and bottom rows, sew 2½" x 2½" print squares to both sides of 2 matching flying geese units from Step 1. Press the seams toward the center. The rows should measure 2½" x 8½".

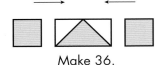

Make 36.

4. For the center row, sew matching flying geese from Step 1 to both sides of square-in-a-square unit from Step 2. Press the seams away from the center. The row should measure 4½" x 8½".

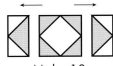

Make 18.

5. Join the rows to complete the blocks. Press the seams away from the center row. The block should measure 8½" x 8½".

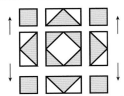

Make 18 positive blocks.

Negative Blocks

6. Using the Two-Square technique, make 68 flying geese from each print 7" x 7" square and background 5½" x 5½" square. The units should measure 2½" x 4½".

Make 68.

7. Make square-in-a-square units from each print 4½" x 4½" square and EITHER 4 background **FCT**s OR 2½" x 2½" **FCS**s. The units should measure 4½" x 4½".

Make 17.

8. For the top and bottom rows, join 2½" x 2½" background squares to both sides of 2 flying geese units from Step 6. Press the seams toward the center. The rows should measure 2½" x 8½".

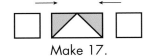

Make 17.

9. For the center rows, join flying geese units from Step 6 to both sides of square-in-a-square units from Step 7. Press the seams away from center. The rows should measure 4½" x 8½".

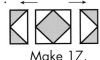

Make 17.

10. Join rows to complete block. Press the seams away from the center row. The blocks should measure 8½" x 8½".

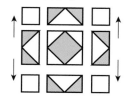

Make 17 negative blocks.

Quilt Assembly

1. Lay out the blocks in 7 rows of 5 blocks each as shown in the quilt assembly diagram. Begin odd numbered rows with a positive block and even numbered rows with a negative block.

2. Sew the blocks into rows. Press seams in alternating directions from row to row. Sew the rows together. Press the seams in one direction. The quilt center needs to measure 40½" x 56½" for the pieced border to fit.

3. Join 5 background 1½" inner border strips end-to-end. Cut 2 side borders 1½" x 56½" and add to the quilt (page 34–36). Cut top and bottom borders 1½" x 42½". Add to the quilt. The quilt center should measure 42½" x 58½".

4. Join 29 print 2½" x 4½" rectangles together to make 2 side borders measuring 4½" x 58½" each. Press the seams in the same direction. Add to the sides.

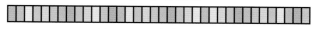

Make 2 side borders.

5. Join 25 print 2½" x 4½" rectangles together to make top and bottom borders measuring 4½" x 50½". Press seams in the same direction. Add to the quilt.

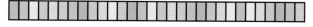

Make 2 top and bottom borders.

6. Layer the quilt top, batting, and backing. Baste the layers together and quilt as desired.

7. Join 6 binding 2½" wide strips end-to-end and apply to the quilt (pages 36–38).

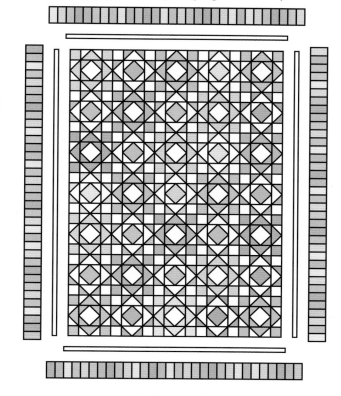

Quilt assembly

TINY TRIANGLES, 5" x 6" and LITTLE PINWHEELS, 8" x 8", both made and quilted by Dianne Yarcho from waste-not, want-not HSTs

Cathy Busch ◆ Newfangled Piecing: Faster & Easier

MELINDA'S GARDEN

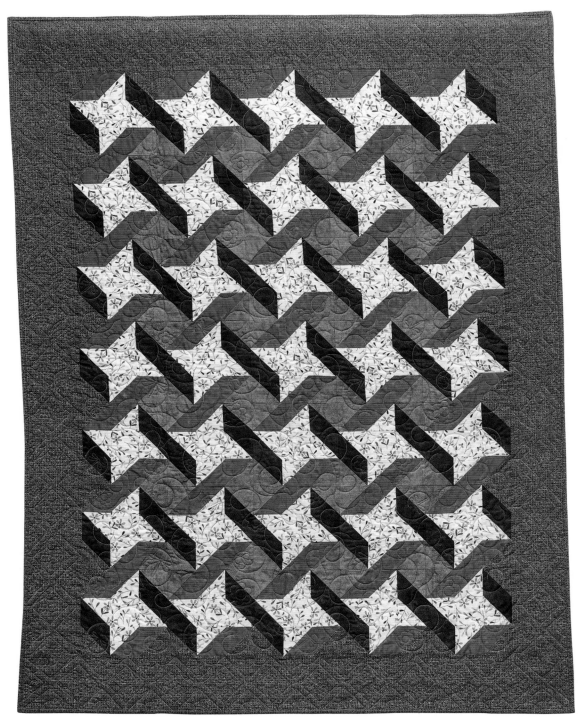

MELINDA'S GARDEN, 47"x 62", made by the author, quilted by Julie Messery, Cedar Falls, Iowa

Cathy Busch ◆ Newfangled Piecing: Faster & Easier

Finished Block Size—7½" x 7½"

The Ribbon Star block is one of my favorite blocks because of its versatility. Color placement changes its look. In this version I selected a light print for the center stars. The two shades of green make the ribbon appear to twist. The orange creates a diagonal trellis for the flower stars.

Yardage

Light floral fabric—
  1 yard (if using the Flip-Corner Triangle technique)
  OR
  1¼ yards (if using the Flip-Corner Square technique)
Orange—1 yard
Dark green—1 yard
Light green—
  ⅝ yard (if using the Flip-Corner Triangle technique)
  OR
  ¾ yard (if using the Flip-Corner Square technique)
Teal (flip corners, border and binding)
  1⅝ yard (if using the Flip-Corner Triangle technique)
  OR
  1¾ yards (if using the Flip-Corner-Square technique)
Backing—3⅞ yards
Batting—55" x 70"

Cutting Instructions

From the light floral fabric:
- Cut 3 strips 3" wide. Cut 35 squares 3" x 3" (block centers).
- Cut 7 strips 3½" wide. Cut 70 squares 3½" x 3½". Cut each square once on the diagonal to make 140 **FCT**s. Cut a 3" x 3" square from cardboard or template plastic. Cut once on

Tip:

- Five different blocks are made from four different parallelograms.

- Blocks are made using partial seam construction (page 13).

- I found it easier to make each of the different parallelograms and put them in a labeled plastic bag. To make the different blocks, simply remove the number of parallelograms needed from the proper bag.

the diagonal to make a marking template.
OR
- For flip-corner squares, cut 11 strips 3" wide. Cut 140 **FCS**s 3" x 3".

From the orange fabric:
- Cut 6 strips 5½" wide. Cut 70 rectangles 3" x 5½".

From the dark green fabric:
- Cut 6 strips 5½" wide. Cut 70 rectangles 3" x 5½".

From the light green fabric:
- For flip-corner triangles, cut 5 strips 3½" wide. Cut 48 squares 3½" x 3½". Cut each square once on the diagonal to make 96 **FCT**s.
OR
- For **FCS**s, cut 8 strips 3" wide. Cut 96 squares 3" x 3".

From the teal fabric:
- Cut 6 strips 5½" wide (border).
- Cut 6 strips 2½" wide (binding).

- For flip-corner triangles, cut 2 strips 3½" wide. Cut 22 squares 3½" x 3½". Cut each square once on the diagonal to make 44 **FCT**s.

OR

- For **FCS**s, cut 4 strips 3" wide. Cut 44 squares 3" x 3".

Sewing Instructions

Parallelogram 1

Note: All the parallelograms are right-flip (page 26) and measure 3" x 5½".

Make 22 parallelograms from orange 3" x 5½" rectangles and EITHER light floral and teal **FCT**s OR 3" x 3" **FCS**s.

Make 22.

Parallelogram 2

Make 48 parallelograms from orange 3" x 5½" rectangles and EITHER light floral and light green **FCT**s OR 3" x 3" **FCS**s.

Make 48.

Parallelogram 3

Make 22 parallelograms from dark green 3" x 5½" rectangles and EITHER teal and light floral **FCT**s OR 3" x 3" **FCS**s.

Make 22.

Parallelogram 4

Make 48 parallelograms from dark green 3" x 5½" rectangles and EITHER light floral and light green **FCT**s OR 3" x 3" **FCS**s.

Make 48.

Block Assembly

Note: The parallelograms are listed in the clockwise sequence in which they are added around the center square, starting from the top, using partial seam construction (page 13). The blocks should measure 8" x 8".

Block #1

Make 2 Block #1 from 3" x 3" light floral squares and parallelograms 1, 3, 2, and 3.

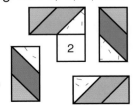

Make 2 Block #1.

Block #2

Make 6 Block #2 from 3" x 3" light floral squares and parallelograms 1, 3, 2, and 4.

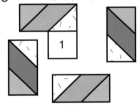

Make 6 Block #2.

Block #3

Make 2 Block #3 from 3" x 3" light floral squares and parallelograms 1, 3, 1, and 4.

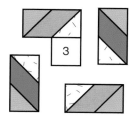

Make 2 Block #3.

Block #4

Make 10 Block #4 from 3" x 3" light floral squares and parallelograms 1, 2, 3, and 4.

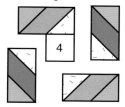

Make 10 Block #4.

Block #5

Make 15 Block #5 from 3" x 3" light floral squares and parallelograms 2, 4, 2, and 4.

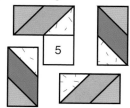

Make 15 Block #5.

Quilt Assembly

1. Arrange the blocks in 7 rows of 5 blocks as indicated in the quilt assembly diagram paying careful attention to the orientation of the blocks.

2. Join the blocks into rows. Press the seams in opposite directions from row to row.

3. Join the rows together. Press the seams in one direction.

4. Join 6 border strips 5½" wide end-to-end. Measure, cut, and add the side borders, then the top and bottom borders (pages 34–36). Press the seams toward the border.

5. Layer the quilt top, batting, and backing. Baste the layers together and quilt as desired.

6. Join 6 binding 2½" wide strips end-to-end and apply to the quilt (pages 36–38).

Quilt assembly

STRETCH STARS AND BARS

STRETCH STARS AND BARS, 39" x 39", made by the author, quilted by Julie Messerly, Cedar Falls, Iowa

Finished Block Size—6" x 6"

Who doesn't love a Star block? By flipping corners on squares and rectangles this Stretch Star block is a snap to make. Add strip-pieced Bars blocks and you have a quick table topper or wallhanging. The 4" blocks in the corners of the border add an extra touch.

Yardage

Background–¾ yard
Dark bars–¼ yard
Light bars–⅜ yard
Red flip corner and inner border–scraps totaling about ½ yard
Outer border and binding–⅞ yard
Backing–2¾ yards (If your backing is wider than 40", 1⅜ yards might be enough.)
Batting–47" x 47"

Cutting Instructions

From the background fabric:
- Cut 2 strips 5" wide. Cut into 26 rectangles 2" x 5". Trim the remainder to 3½" wide and cut 8 squares 3½" x 3½".
- Cut 2 strips 3½" wide. Cut an additional 5 squares 3½" x 3½" (13 total), 26 rectangles 2" x 3½", and 7 rectangles 1½" x 3½".
- Cut 1 strip 2½" wide. Cut into 4 squares 2½" x 2½", 8 rectangles 1½" x 2½", and 9 squares 2" x 2".
- Cut 1 strip 2" wide. Cut an additional 17 squares 2" x 2" (26 total).
- Cut 1 strip 1½" wide. Cut into 8 squares 1½" x 1½" and 1 additional rectangle 1½" x 3½" (8 total).

Tips:

- For a quick baby quilt, use bright or pastel fabrics for the star points and a juvenile print for the borders.

- Match the star center and point fabric for a completely different look. Use a 3½" preprinted square or fussy cut motif for the star centers

- 32 Stretch Star blocks and 31 Bars blocks make a 42" x 54" quilt center. Add 4½" borders for a snuggly lap quilt.

From the dark bar fabric:
- Cut 4 strips 2" wide.

From the light bar fabric:
- Cut 6 strips 1½" wide.

From the red fabric scraps:
- For the Star block flip-corner triangles, cut 39 squares 2½" x 2½". Cut each square once on the diagonal to make 78 **FCT**s. Cut a 2" x 2" square from cardboard or template plastic. Cut once on the diagonal to make a marking template.

AND
- For the corner block flip-corner triangles, cut 12 squares 2" x 2". Cut each square once on the diagonal to make 24 **FCT**s. Cut a 1½" x 1½" square from cardboard or template plastic. Cut once on the diagonal to make a marking template (for the corner Star blocks).

OR
- For the Star block flip-corner squares, cut 78 **FCS**s 2" x 2".

AND

- For the corner block flip-corner squares, cut 24 **FCS**s 1½" x 1½".
- Cut random length pieces 1¼" wide. Join pieces end-to-end using either straight or 45-degree seams to make a strip about 130" long (for the inner border).

From the outer border and binding fabric:

- Cut 4 strips 4½" wide (border).
- Cut 4 strips 2½" wide (binding).

Sewing Instructions

1. Make 2 strip-sets alternating 3 light bar 1½" strips and 2 dark bar 2" strips. Press toward the dark strips. The strip-set should measure 6½" wide.

2. Cut into 12 squares 6½" x 6½" for the Bars blocks.

 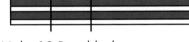

6½"

Make 12 Bars blocks.

3. Make 13 alternate flip-corner squares (page 27) from the background 3½" x 3½" squares and EITHER the large red **FCT**s OR 2½" x 2½" **FCS**s. The units should measure 3½" x 3½".

Make 13.

4. Make 26 right flip-corner units from 2" x 3½" background rectangles and EITHER large red **FCT**s OR 2" x 2" **FCS**s.

Make 26.

5. Join the units from Step 3 to the top and bottom of each unit from Step 2. Press the seams toward the center. The units should measure 6½" x 3½".

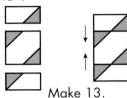

Make 13.

6. Make 26 left flip-corner units from 2" x 5" background rectangles and EITHER large red **FCT**s OR 2" x 2" **FCS**s.

Make 26.

7. Add 2" x 2" background squares to the flip-corner end of each unit from Step 6. Press the seams toward the square. The units should measure 2" x 6½".

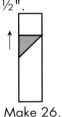

Make 26.

8. Add the units from Step 7 to the sides of the center units from Step 5 to complete the blocks. Press the seams away from the center. The blocks should measure 6½" x 6½".

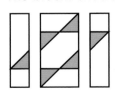

Make 13 Star blocks.

Make 4 corner Star blocks referring to the figures for the large stars.

a. Make 4 alternate flip-corner squares from the 2½" x 2½" background squares and EITHER the small red **FCT**s OR 1½" x 1½" **FCS**s (see step 3).

b. Make 8 right flip-corner units from 1½ x 2½ background rectangles and EITHER small red **FCT**s OR 1½" x 1½" **FCS**s (see step 4).

c. Join the units from Step a and Step b (see step 5). Press the seams toward the center. The units should measure 2½" x 4½".

d. Make 8 left flip-corner units from 1½" x 3½" background rectangles and EITHER small red **FCT**s OR 1½" x 1½" **FCS**s (see step 6).

e. Add a 1½" x 1½" square to the flip-corner end of the Step d rectangles (see step 7). Press the seams toward the square. The units should measure 1½" x 4½".

f. Add the side units from Step e to the sides of the block centers from Step c (see step 8). Press the seams away from the center. The blocks should measure 4½" x 4½".

Make 4 corner Stretch Star blocks.

Quilt Assembly

1. Arrange 13 Star blocks and 12 Bars blocks as indicated in the quilt assembly diagram or in your own design.

2. Sew the blocks into rows. Press the seams toward the Bars blocks.

3. Join the rows together to make the quilt center. Press the seams in one direction.

4. Measure and cut side inner borders from the 1¼" wide pieced inner-border strip (pages 34–36). Add to the quilt. Repeat for the top and bottom inner borders.

5. Measure and cut the top and bottom borders from the 4½" wide border strips. Sew corner Star blocks to both ends of the border strips. Press toward the border strips.

6. Measure the length of quilt. Cut side borders from the 4½" wide border strips. Add the side borders. Press the seams toward the border.

7. Add the top and bottom borders. Press the seams toward the border.

8. Layer the quilt top, batting, and backing. Baste the layers together and quilt as desired.

Join 4 binding strips 2½" wide and apply to the quilt (pages 36–38).

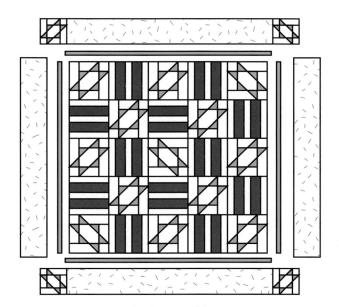

Quilt assembly

Numbers Every Quilter Should Know

Fraction Decimal Equivalents

Fraction	$\frac{1}{8}$	$\frac{1}{4}$	$\frac{3}{8}$	$\frac{1}{2}$	$\frac{5}{8}$	$\frac{3}{4}$	$\frac{7}{8}$
Decimal	.125	.25	.375	.5	.625	.75	.875
Portion of a Yard in Inches	4½"	9"	13½"	18"	22½"	27"	31½"

Squares per 40" Strip of Fabric

1"	40	1¼"	32	1½"	26	1¾"	22
2"	20	2¼"	17	2½"	16	2¾"	14
3"	13	3¼"	12	3½"	11	3¾"	10
4"	10	4¼"	9	4½"	8	4¾"	8
5"	8	5¼"	7	5½"	7	5¾"	6
6"	6	6¼"	6	6½"	6	6¾"	6
7"	5	7¼"	5	7½"	5	7¾"	5
8"	5	8¼"	4	8½"	4	8¾"	4
9"	4	9¼"	4	9½"	4	9¾"	4
10"	4	10¼"	3	10½"	3	10¾"	3

Squares per Fat Quarter (18" x 20")

1"	360	1¼"	224	1½"	156	1¾"	110
2"	90	2¼"	64	2½"	56	2¾"	42
3"	36	3¼"	30	3½"	25	3¾"	20
4"	20	4¼"	16	4½"	16	4¾"	12
5"	9	5¼"	12	5½"	9	5¾"	9
6"	9	6¼"	6	6½"	6	6¾"	6
7"	6	7¼"	4	7½"	4	7¾"	4
8"	4	8¼"	4	8½"	4	8¾"	4
9"	4	9¼"	2	9½"	2	9¾"	2
10"	2	10¼"	1	10½"	1	10¾"	1

Quilt Sizes

	Crib	Twin	Double	Queen	King
Quilt Size	36" x 54"	54" x 90"	72" x 90"	90" x 108"	108" x 108"
Mattress	27" x 52"	39" x 75"	54" x 75"	60" x 80"	76" x 80"
Batting	45" x 60"	72" x 90"	80" x 96"	90" x 108"	120" x 120"

Cutting Sizes for Side and Corner Setting Triangles

Finished Size	Finished Diagonal	Cut Size for Side Setting Triangles [insert one-diagonal-cut icon]	Cut Size for Corner Setting Triangles [insert two-diagonal-cuts icon]
1"	$1\frac{3}{8}$"	$1\frac{5}{8}$" x $1\frac{5}{8}$"	$2\frac{3}{4}$" x $2\frac{3}{4}$"
$1\frac{1}{2}$"	$2\frac{1}{8}$"	$3\frac{3}{8}$" x $3\frac{3}{8}$"	2" x 2"
2"	$2\frac{7}{8}$"	$4\frac{1}{8}$" x $4\frac{1}{8}$"	$2\frac{3}{8}$" x $2\frac{3}{8}$"
$2\frac{1}{2}$"	$3\frac{1}{2}$"	$4\frac{7}{8}$" x $4\frac{7}{8}$"	$2\frac{3}{4}$" x $2\frac{3}{4}$"
3"	$4\frac{1}{4}$"	$5\frac{1}{2}$" x $5\frac{1}{2}$"	3" x 3"
$3\frac{1}{2}$"	5"	$6\frac{1}{4}$" x $6\frac{1}{4}$"	$3\frac{3}{8}$" x $3\frac{3}{8}$"
4"	$5\frac{5}{8}$"	7" x 7"	$3\frac{3}{4}$" x $3\frac{3}{4}$"
$4\frac{1}{2}$"	$6\frac{3}{8}$"	$7\frac{5}{8}$" x $7\frac{5}{8}$"	$4\frac{1}{8}$" x $4\frac{1}{8}$"
5"	$7\frac{1}{8}$"	$8\frac{3}{8}$" x $8\frac{3}{8}$"	$4\frac{1}{2}$" x $4\frac{1}{2}$"
$5\frac{1}{2}$"	$7\frac{3}{4}$"	$9\frac{3}{8}$" x $9\frac{3}{8}$"	$4\frac{7}{8}$" x $4\frac{7}{8}$"
6"	$8\frac{1}{2}$"	$9\frac{3}{4}$" x $9\frac{3}{4}$"	$5\frac{1}{8}$" x $5\frac{1}{8}$"
$6\frac{1}{2}$"	$9\frac{1}{4}$"	$10\frac{1}{2}$" x $10\frac{1}{2}$"	$5\frac{1}{2}$" x $5\frac{1}{2}$"
7"	$9\frac{7}{8}$"	$11\frac{1}{4}$" x $11\frac{1}{4}$"	$5\frac{7}{8}$" x $5\frac{7}{8}$"
$7\frac{1}{2}$"	$10\frac{5}{8}$"	$11\frac{7}{8}$" x $11\frac{7}{8}$"	$6\frac{1}{4}$" x $6\frac{1}{4}$"
8"	$11\frac{3}{8}$"	$12\frac{5}{8}$" x $12\frac{5}{8}$"	$6\frac{5}{8}$" x $6\frac{5}{8}$"
$8\frac{1}{2}$"	12"	$13\frac{3}{8}$" x $13\frac{3}{8}$"	7" x 7"
9"	$12\frac{3}{4}$"	14" x 14"	$7\frac{1}{4}$" x $7\frac{1}{4}$"
$9\frac{1}{2}$"	$13\frac{3}{8}$"	$14\frac{3}{4}$" x $14\frac{3}{4}$"	$7\frac{5}{8}$" x $7\frac{5}{8}$"
10"	$14\frac{1}{8}$"	$15\frac{1}{2}$" x $15\frac{1}{2}$"	8" x 8"
$10\frac{1}{2}$"	$14\frac{7}{8}$"	$16\frac{1}{8}$" x $16\frac{1}{8}$"	$8\frac{3}{8}$" x $8\frac{3}{8}$"
11"	$15\frac{1}{2}$"	$16\frac{7}{8}$" x $16\frac{7}{8}$"	$8\frac{3}{4}$" x $8\frac{3}{4}$"
$11\frac{1}{2}$"	$16\frac{1}{4}$"	$17\frac{5}{8}$" x $17\frac{5}{8}$"	$9\frac{1}{8}$" x $9\frac{1}{8}$"
12"	17"	$18\frac{1}{4}$" x $18\frac{1}{4}$"	$9\frac{3}{8}$" x $9\frac{3}{8}$"

Formulas

Side setting triangles—finished size x 1.414 + 1.25
Corner setting triangles—finished size ÷ 1.414 + .875
Round the result up to the nearest $\frac{1}{4}$".

◆ Eliminate Seams to Simplify Blocks

Eliminating seams requires calculating the cut size of the replacement unit. The calculations are easy or refer to the charts.

Step 1 -   Determine the finished size of the block.
Step 2 -   Count the number of squares per row in the block.
Step 3 -   Divide the finished size (Step 1) of the block by the number of squares (Step 2).
Step 4 -   Add 1 to the number of seams being eliminated.
Step 5 -   Multiply Step 3 x Step 4 and add ½" to determine cut length.

Example: 12" block, 3 squares per row, 12"÷3=4", eliminating one seam, 1+1=2, 4" x 2=8"+½"= 8½" long x 4½" wide cut size.

Example: 8" block, 4 squares per row, 8"÷4 = 2", eliminating two seams 1+2=3, 2" x 3=6"+½" = 6½" long x 2½" wide cut size.

Nine-Patch Block: 3 squares per row, 3 rows per block

Block Size	3"	4½"	6"	7½"	9"	10½"	12"
Finished Block	1"	1½"	2"	2½"	3"	3½"	4"
Eliminate 1 Seam	1½" x 2½"	2" x 3"	2½" x 4½"	3" x 5½"	3½" x 6½"	4" x 7½"	4½" x 8½"
Eliminate 2 Seams	1½" x 3½"	2" x 4½"	2½" x 6½"	3" x 8"	3½" x 9½"	4" x 11"	4½" x 12½"

16-Patch Block: 4 squares per row, 4 rows per block

Block Size	4"	6"	8"	10"	12"
Finished Block	1"	1½"	2"	2½"	3"
Eliminate 1 Seam	1½" x 2½"	2" x 3½"	2½" x 4½"	3" x 5½"	3½" x 6½"
Eliminate 2 Seams	1½" x 3½"	2" x 5"	2½" x 6½"	3" x 8"	3½" x 9½"
Eliminate 3 Seams	1½" x 4½"	2" x 6½"	2½" x 8½"	3" x 10½"	3½" x 12½"

25-Patch Block: 5 squares per row, 5 rows per block

Block Size	4"	7½"	10"	12½"
Finished Block	1"	1½"	2"	2½"
Eliminate 1 Seam	1½" x 2½"	2" x 3½"	2½" x 4½"	3" x 5½"
Eliminate 2 Seams	1½" x 3½"	2" x 5"	2½" x 6½"	3" x 8 "
Eliminate 3 Seams	1½" x 4½"	2" x 6½"	2½" x 8½"	3" x 10½"
Eliminate 4 Seams	1½" x 5½"	2" x 8"	2½" x 10½"	3" x 13"

Seams can also be eliminated by combining small squares to make one large square. Multiply the finished size of the small squares by the number of squares to be replaced and add ½".

Example combining 4 squares with a 3" finished size to make 1 large square.
(3" x 2) + 6" = ½" = 6½". The replacement square is cut 6½" x 6½".

◈ Meet Cathy Busch

I grew up in Euclid, Ohio. After school, I would spend time with a neighbor, Mrs. Miller. She was a seamstress, but she never taught me how to sew. My job was to string buttons.

She must have had every button in the world. She would hand me a double-threaded needle and a tin of buttons. At first I would just take a button from the tin and put it on the string at random. Later I'd sort the buttons by color, by shape, or by the number of holes before stringing them. Even after I realized that as soon as I left she'd cut the string and return the buttons to the tin, I still enjoyed developing new sorting systems for stringing the buttons.

This early experience in classification and organization contributed to two bachelor of education degrees and a masters in mathematics education. During my junior year at Bowling Green State University, my major professor introduced me to his new graduate student—a tall, blond, handsome guy from a small town in Iowa. We eventually married and, after living in Oregon and Arizona, we returned to his hometown of Waverly, Iowa.

I tried my hand at several crafts—knitting, crocheting, counted cross-stitch, and macramé. About seventeen years ago I made a series of counted cross-stitch bears. My husband was working on a fundraiser and suggested I sew the bears together and make a blanket for the auction. Not knowing what I was doing, I asked the local church ladies for help. The next thing I knew, I was a first-generation quilter.

I joined guilds, started a stash, and began taking classes. His suggestion became my addiction. In quilting, I found a way to combine my love of mathematics and a creative outlet. I was drawn to traditional pieced blocks and finding ways to adapt the blocks to create unique quilts.

My quilts have been juried into a number of national shows and I have won local and state awards for my quilts. My Iowa Sesquicentennial Challenge quilt, WAITING, won Best of Category and traveled throughout the country. In addition, I've written several articles for Fons and Porter's *Love of Quilting* magazine.

As mentors increased my knowledge, I began to share my knowledge with others. My programs range from the technical to the humorous aspects of quilting. My workshops are designed with a technical component while strongly encouraging participants to explore their creativity.

Whether taking or teaching classes, I believe a bad day quilting is better than a good day doing anything else.

More AQS Books

This is only a small selection of the books available from the American Quilter's Society. AQS books are known worldwide for timely topics, clear writing, beautiful color photos, and accurate illustrations and patterns. The following books are available from your local bookseller, quilt shop, or public library.

#1417

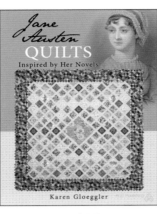

#1415

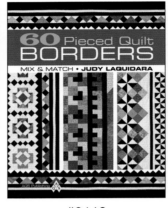

#8662

#8663

#1246

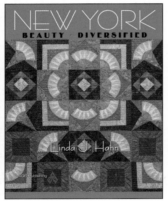

#1251

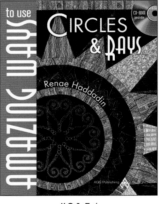

#8154

#8761

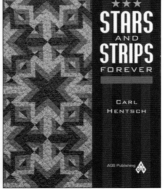

#1245